CORRIDORS OF PA ...

CORRIDORS OF PAUA

*The story of New Zealand's
decline into world leadership*

A. K. Grant

Illustrated by Tom Scott
with unused colourings-in
by A. K. Grant

HAZARD PRESS
publishers

For Jane and Averil,
with our love

First published 1996
Text copyright © 1996 A. K. Grant
Illustrations copyright © 1996 Tom Scott

ISBN 0-908790-98-8

Published by Hazard Press
P.O. Box 2151, Christchurch, New Zealand
Production and design by Orca Publishing Services Ltd
Back cover photo of Tom Scott by Annelies Van Der Poel
Back cover photo of A.K. Grant by Rob Tucker

Printed in New Zealand

Contents

Introduction

By Jean-Paul Sinartre
Lecteur, Philosophe et Savant-Général
Lycée Au Contraire
Paris

As a leading French philosopher, who translates all his own works into English rather than trust an Englishman to do so, I often despair of *les Anglais* (an untranslatable term of contempt). But I am proud to be associated with this work because Messieurs Grant and Scott have invented a school of historical writing that entirely accords with my own metaphysics. I call this new form of historical writing 'History-As-Feeling'. It involves a sublime indifference to the facts, provided that the emotions which those facts engender are accurately recorded. M. Grant, with his antique typewriting mechanism, M. Scott with his pencil and nib, are recreating history as a *craft*, akin to woollen wall-hangings or terracotta garden pots with strange protuberances. Thus they render themselves impervious to the criticism of so-called scholars, capable of little more than playing SEGA games upon their PC screens. As I lie in the arms of Michelle, my research assistant, I hear the thunderous clatter of M. Grant's typewriter and the scratch of M. Scott's nib; and I hear muttered imprecations as M. Grant commits another typo and M. Scott deposits a blot on his expensive drawing-paper. Clio, the Muse of history, is in every way a woman: she yields her secrets and her joys only to those who respect her. Messieurs Grant and Scott have proved their respect for Clio in this book: they have taken her out for dinner and then dropped her off at her own door without even coming in for coffee. As Clio takes her mug of Nescafé to her lonely bed, she knows she has been respected by experts. She and I salute them.

J-P Sinartre
Rue de 12 octobre
Paris, 1996

Chapter One

The Natives are Restless

*A*t 6.45 on the morning of 13 July 1984, the alarm bell rang at the bedside of George Cross-winning fireman, Tony Matstic. The morning light was flooding through the curtains of his Island Bay home. With the grace of an athlete, he silenced the alarm, and moved on to the fair white body of his wife, Elena. Within moments, she began to respond.

Across the sleeping city of Wellington, garage forecourt attendant Hemi Pakaitori pumped 25 litres into a Government Service Garage LTD. He recognised the plump, bespectacled figure in the rear of the opulent vehicle, wolfing a Georgie Pie. 'Jeez,' he thought. 'That David Lange's up early. What's going on?'

In Washington, American Secretary of State George P. Schultz had his phone swept to make sure it wasn't still being bugged by Henry Kissinger, and then barked down the line. 'What the hell's going on down there in Wellington?' he rasped, with all the authority of command. 'Has Robin Muldoon got it sewn up or what?'

And at the CIA listening station in Pine Gap, Australia, traffic was unusually heavy.

As was the cumbersome Morrison reel mower being wheeled across a lawn in Birkenhead, Auckland, by Sidney Beverage, 72, a pensioner who could not sleep. Neighbours redrafted, in their minds, the sulphurous letters to the council that were somehow never sent.

But all this is irrelevant, because the election that was to change the course of world history, the New Zealand election of 14 July 1984, did not take place till the following day.

It is not given to every small country to effect, by democratic means, a radical shift in the tectonic plates of world history. But that mantle descended upon the shoulders of the New Zealand electorate on 14 July 1984. Few electors, let alone politicians, realised that such an earthquake was about to take place. One who did was Labour Finance spokesman Roger Douglas.

Douglas was about to unleash upon the country the hot blast of free-market economics – to loosen the stays of control and allow the belly and breasts of the economy to support themselves without regulatory underwear. No one, least of all the Labour Party and certainly not the Labour voters, knew that Douglas's mind was a ferment of Friedman and Hayek: not a New York law firm but an economist and philosopher respectively. They had already given Ronald Reagan and Margaret Thatcher something to live for, and Douglas's version of them would become known as Rogernomics, i.e. a system in which the economy is rogered. To grasp what it was that Douglas had in mind, let us examine the salient features of the free market, as it operates in a small economy.

1. The best things in life are free-market

The best things in life, from a Rogernomical point of view, are expensive cars, expensive houses, expensive women and expense accounts. These are best provided by an economy in which government regulation plays little or no part. Rugby provides an apt analogy. In free-market rugby the government would paint the white lines and provide the goalposts, but there would be no referee. Jersey-pulling, eye-gouging and head-stomping would be permitted because they were not prohibited, and injured players would have to find their own way to the St John Ambulance officers, who would not be permitted to run on to the field. The game would be played during all the hours that God sends, and there would be as many teams as there was room for on the paddock.

2. Government should not own anything apart from ministerial LTDs and a couple of Skyhawks

In other words, if the government owned a profitable asset, it should disencumber itself of it forthwith, so that its friends could make a profit out of it instead. Thus railways, the electricity system, the telephone system, the national airline, Government Print, the postal

BELIEVE ME, THIS IS GOING TO HURT ME MORE THAN IT HURTS YOU...

service, parts of the health service, Petrocorp, *pinus radiata* forests, the BNZ – all should pass into private hands, in deals suggested by merchant banks, brokered by merchant banks, and with merchant banks often acquiring a healthy slice of the action. The Inland Revenue would not be sold as such, but would be leased out to the Cook Islands.

These sales would reduce the national debt. They would also reduce the government's income, though not the incomes of those who acquired the assets at 'Save! Save! Save! Dollars! Dollars! Dollars!' prices. But Douglas wasn't worried about the loss of government revenue because he had a new scheme hidden behind the socks in his policy drawer – GST. He certainly wasn't going to tell the electorate about this revolutionary revenue, and very wisely, because when the Liberals made it a platform plank in the 1993 Australian election they got done like a dinner. In New Zealand they would have had to pay GST on the dinner they got done like.

3. *In she comes and out she goes*
In other words, capital inflows and outflows should be unregulated. Companies should be free to borrow offshore and New Zealanders should be free to buy as many piastres and zlotys as they wished. Imports should be uncontrolled: Japanese cars, Lalique glassware and Chinese shirts should flow across our borders and be paid for by the burgeoning export sector. The burgeoning export sector would, however, receive no government

subsidies or other protection and would learn to stand on its own two feet: in the case of sheepfarmers and clothing manufacturers, on their two bare feet. Still there would very soon be far fewer lambs cluttering up the countryside, meaning more grass for all.

New forms of life, such as forex dealers and futures traders, would emerge blinking into the Rogernomian sunlight, while the average Kiwi scuttled about on the forest floor, bumping into things and trying to avoid predators.

4. Welfare, Schmelfare!

Or, in other words, why should rich people have to pay to educate other people's children, or pay for hospitals full of sick people they were never likely to meet socially? To the free marketeer, dependency on welfare was a sign of moral infirmity, lack of vigour, or an unsettling reminder of the bad luck which haunted their own dreams. The best way to put those people out of mind was to plaster the property with security lights, build a high fence, and abolish the welfare state. In the fifty years between 1935 and 1985, New Zealanders had constructed a welfare state that they took for granted, largely because they assumed they were paying for it themselves. 'Not so,' cried the rich and their humble but influential ayatollahs in Treasury, 'it is being paid for by punitive taxation and overseas borrowing.'

There was something in this but, as we shall see, overseas borrowing soared while the paternalistic state paled, and grew spectre-thin, and died.

All this was in the future in July 1984, at the same time only a matter of moments away. It is now time to examine how 'les événements' of July 1984 came about.

The Doon of Muldoom (a 'literal' there, as we authors say, but let it stand)

For eight and a half years New Zealand had shivered in the iron grip of Rob Muldoon, the nearest thing we ever had in New Zealand to a Bosnian Serb Prime Minister. His reign has been chronicled in our previous book, *The Paua and the Glory*, a work essential to any understanding of our island story. It is now, alas, out of print, and the unsigned copies are very valuable (it is rumoured that Alan Gibbs, noted collector, has forty of them in a special case in his library). Suffice it to say for present purposes that in June 1984 Muldoon, corrupted by absolute power, went mad and called a snap election. He drove, drunk, to Government House (perhaps the most dramatic piece of drunken driving in our history, though it is fair to state that Muldoon himself was not behind the wheel), and demanded a dissolution, a condition in which he was increasingly finding himself. His imperious request was acceded to by a bemused, or maybe only amused, Governor-General, and the seeds of Muldoon's downfall were sown.

Labour, Poised Like an Elephant, Ready to Spring

The real phrase is, of course, 'Labour, Poised Like a Tiger, Ready to Spring', but (a) it wasn't spring, it was the middle of winter, and (b) the tiger was Douglas, lurking behind the large toenails on the enormous flat feet of David Lange, the Labour elephant, whose

trunk suddenly erected itself and sniffed the scent of victory. What suddenly caused this tumescence? Why, nothing other than the slim, girlish figure of Marilyn Waring.

What Was Marilyn Waring?

The mantle of the anti-nuclear crusader. She had advised Muldoon that she would support him on matters of confidence and supply, but would support Labour on the barring of nuclear-armed or powered vessels from the saline but unirradiated waters of our pristine harbours.

The legislation, sponsored by the unlikely combination of Richard Prebble and Helen Clark – plus Marilyn, appeared likely to achieve its passage, unlike the next American nuclear submarine. For some reason, seemingly a combination of alcohol, diabetes and sheer pique, Muldoon could not stomach defeat on this fairly peripheral issue: hence the midnight dash to Government House. When Waring announced that she would not support the government on its pro-nuclear policy, she was howled down in the House and burst into tears. They turned out to be bitter tears indeed, and it would have been

THEN AND NOW...

N.Z.
FIRST COUNTRY IN THE WORLD TO INTRODUCE WOMENS SUFFRAGE, OLD AGE PENSIONS, THE FORTY HOUR WEEK, AND THE WELFARE STATE

WORLDS FASTEST GROWING GAP BETWEEN RICH AND POOR

better for the National Party if Muldoon had shed them himself, and gone back to Vogel instead of Government House. But Rob was not the man to allow a waif-like figure such as Marilyn Waring to unzip his fly and allow the electorate, let alone the Americans, catch sight of the wizened political walnut which lay beneath it.

The People's Voice Is Heard

The people's voice *was* heard, but only somewhat belatedly, after people woke up to the fact that under our constitution it was permitted, by law, to vote against Muldoon. One man who alerted people to this fact was the property millionaire, later Baron Jones of Melling, who founded the New Zealand Party, comprised of murderers like Ron Jorgensen and pretty women who were mostly called Georgina. Jones, once an ardent supporter of Muldoon, had turned against him; and cowed New Zealanders, seeing a very rich man raise his voice against the Tamaki Tamburlaine, realised that even people on quarter-acre sections might be allowed to do the same. And they did. With consequences they could not have imagined:

(a) the collapse of ANZUS
(b) the collapse of the New Zealand dollar
(c) nothing much else until Roger unleashed the rottweilers of Treasury upon the farmers, the public service, the Cabinet, people who wanted to post a letter, the Cabinet, people who wanted to use the post office to pay bills and pick up

their entitlements, people who thought the government was of the people and for the people, manufacturers, the Cabinet, David Lange, lucrative public enterprises, people employed by the same, the Cabinet, journalists trying to work out what the hell was going on, and, of course, the Cabinet.

An enormous amount of our history occurred in the few days after the election. They deserve a chapter to themselves. But before we devote ourselves to the adrenalin rush of those days which shook the world, let us not forget the immortal, yet tremulous words of Maisie Kilburnie, the Laureate of Lumsden, composed on the morn of the Labour landslide:

> The rain came pitter-patter through my curtain
> Because I hadn't left my window closed:
> But I was feeling rather sort of certain
> An era in our history had closed.
>
> No more the drear, dark, dank days of Sir Robert,
> When Think Big thoughts had made our land a debtor.
> I leafed the gentle pages of *The Hobbit*,
> And thought, 'My word! Things can only get better!
>
> 'The poor will now be cared for, and be cherished;
> The businessmen will get a dire comeuppance,
> And greed and selfishness will soon be perished,
> And benefits go up by one-and-tuppence.[1]
>
> 'Or maybe more; a government that's caring
> Will redistribute co-dependent things,
> And show that on its sleeve its heart it's wearing,
> And once again I'll read *Lord of the Rings*.'

Her references to Tolkien are eloquent reminders of the last hopes of a literate Labour generation. And she spoke for more than she knew, especially as her poem was rejected by the *Tuatapere Clarion, Islands, Mate,* the *Listener,* and, unforgivably, the *Virago Book of Neglected Poetry by Women.* But it was her younger sister, Iris, who, staring into the sullen Southland sky, remarked, 'I do believe, Maisie, that it is quite on the cards that a hard rain's a-gonna fall.'

---

1. Maisie never fully adjusted to decimal currency.

Chapter Two

Standing Up to the Dictators

New Zealand does not enjoy many constitutional crises, mainly because we haven't got anything much resembling a constitution, apart from a few scrawny scraps of legislation, which bear as much resemblance to a constitution as one vertebra and a toe bone would bear to the fleshly envelope which once housed them. But in July 1984 we enjoyed two crises; one constitutional, centring round devaluation, and one international, imperilling the defence of the Western world. The constitutional crisis began at 9pm on Sunday 15 July, when the Reserve Bank suspended trading in foreign currency, because vast capital outflows threatened national bankruptcy. In those far-off days all forex dealings were done through the Reserve Bank, and no one was allowed to participate unless they were (a) holders of import licences; (b) exporters repatriating funds; (c) the Reserve Bank itself; (d) numerous ad hoc exceptions to the above. For some days the Reserve Bank and Treasury had been urging Muldoon to undertake a devaluation. Muldoon rejected this advice because it contained what he termed 'certain discrepancies', i.e. it didn't accord with his own views and was opposed to everything he stood for, whatever that was. Instead he insisted that Lange, the Prime Minister-elect, should join him in a declaration that there would be no devaluation. This, he felt, would restore confidence, not least in his own policies, and prove to the world that the New Zealand economy still danced, or rather, jerked, to his bidding.

Lange wasn't having a bar of this and got very angry. The problem was that until certain documents called 'writs' were returned to some obscure official, Muldoon's government was still in office. Labour could not be sworn in until the elusive writs turned up in the mail. And it was no good going down to check the letterbox hourly, because the writs were not going to arrive for days, if not weeks. And until they did, National was a 'caretaker administration': a gross misnomer since Muldoon was behaving as if he were still the headmaster rather than the caretaker. But nothing could be done without his fiat (actually a Ford Sierra).

What was to be done, while the nation's reserves dwindled and Muldoon's ego expanded? No one knew, least of all the National Cabinet. They had never come across such a situation before; someone telling the Boss to do something he ought, but didn't want, to do.

They met on the night of Monday 16 July and resolved to replace Muldoon; the problem was, with whom? They had all been emasculated by Sir Robert over the years, and fed by him on a special diet which left no chalk in their spines. None was willing to drink of the poisoned chalice of leadership. Matters drifted into Tuesday, when at last the ageing pit bull released his grip on the leg of the body politic. He agreed to water down the currency he had so fiercely defended, and a devaluation of 20 per cent was announced on Wednesday 18 July. Church bells pealed across the land, bonfires were lit along the coasts and money came pouring back with the same alacrity with which it had departed. Where had it gone in the meantime? No one would ever know. 'Offshore' was the closest answer anyone could come up with, and nobody knew where that was either.

What lessons do we learn from this crisis? None, except that Prime Ministers like Muldoon are never defeated until escorted to and from Government House by members of the Armed Offenders Squad. A similar crisis will not occur again, because nowadays our currency rises and falls like the plunger in a toilet cistern. And because of MMP, future Cabinets are unlikely to be so completely dominated by one man. This is good for the country but bad for satirists. The next tyrant, if there is one, will be taller, better looking, and wear pantyhose.

Is this the place to pause for a moment and assess, in a sober and scholarly fashion, the Muldoon legacy, the Muldoon character, the ubiquitous Muldoon piggy-bank? Is it appropriate to consider the forces which shaped him, the motives which drove him, the numerous unacknowledged acts of kindness he performed? To hell with the old bastard. Let someone else do that.

Warlike Councils

At the same time that Lange's nascent administration was standing up to a very short man, it was also standing up to a very tall one. George P. Schultz, American Secretary of State, was in Wellington for a meeting of the ANZUS Council. ANZUS was the allegedly defensive alliance with America into which New Zealand and Australia had entered in 1951. You could hardly blame the government of the day for doing so, even though it was Sid Holland's government. The Americans had undoubtedly saved us during the war, and the British undoubtedly had not, even though our own troops were regularly committed by Churchill and his generals to several disasters in Greece, Crete and the Western Desert. The sinking of the *Prince of Wales* and the *Repulse* and the subsequent fall of Singapore left many New Zealanders looking very thoughtful as they contemplated the frayed bonds of Empire.

In many ways the frenzy for all that 'Home' represented was at its height in the 50s, but it was fueled by guilt, like that of the smallest child in the playground abandoning a failed protector and attaching himself to the biggest of the big boys. We went mad when our slim and lovely Queen came out to visit us in 1953; no single visitor to our shores has ever been the recipient of so much adolescent yearning, most of it from middle-aged men. She was 'radiant'; the word was used a million times. Presumably at night, in bed with the Duke, she glowed in the dark. But to fantasise along such lines would have been treason; the Queen was the most spectacularly chaste sex symbol the Empire had ever known, certainly far more so than her uncle, Edward VIII, her great-grandfather, Edward VII, or her great-great-grandmother, Victoria, who was hardly ever off her back when Albert was alive.

And so during the 50s and 60s we remained united by bonds of fealty to Britain, but in the world of *Realpolitik* we did whatever Washington told Canberra to tell Wellington to do. We sent troops to Vietnam and were visited by Lyndon Johnson, who did not evoke the same reverence as the Queen, except among National Cabinet Ministers. And pursuant to our ANZUS obligations we accepted visits from nuclear-armed and powered ships and submarines. These became increasingly unpopular, except among the sex workers of Karangahape Road and Vivian Street, and were opposed by the daring yachties of the Waitemata and Port Nicholson. And in due course by the Labour Party, which adopted a policy of opposition to such visits. At the time of the '84 election it was not clear whether Lange was as fervent in his opposition to such visits as was the party he led. Nevertheless the Prebble/Clark/Waring anti-nuclear legislation greatly alarmed the Americans, who refused to confirm or deny that their ships were nuclear-armed. Since there was no point to them if they weren't, the American coyness on the point seemed to many a little strange; it was a bit like being visited by a member of the Mongrel Mob who

refused to confirm or deny that there were shells in his sawn-off shotgun but insisted on coming in for a look round anyway.

The Americans, however, were emphatic that if they were forced either to confirm or deny, the Red Army would roll across the plains of North Germany while missiles darkened the skies above North America. Strength in Wellington would be perceived as weakness in the West, and NATO would unravel because an American warship bristling with nuclear weaponry would be acknowledged to be an American warship bristling with nuclear weaponry. Since the whole point of the theory of nuclear deterrence was supposed to be that the enemy knew you *had* the deterrent, it is hard to know what the Americans were on about. Presumably it had to do with the American belief that an ally was there to have its butt kicked, not to ask impertinent questions about what might be concealed in yours.

Anyway, there was much alarm in Washington as the '84 election neared. As chance would have it, a meeting of ANZUS ministers had long been scheduled in Wellington for the week following the election. And so it came about that Schultz met the newly victorious Lange in Wellington on the night of Sunday 15 July, the same night the Reserve Bank suspended trading. He sought assurances about Labour's attitude to ANZUS in general and ship visits in particular. Lange parried such requests with a statement which, like most of Lange's statements, meant less than it sounded as though it meant. 'Mr Secretary,' Lange boomed, 'our two great nations are indissolubly linked by the twin polarities of dissonance.'

Schultz immediately had the statement run through the CIA computers at Langley, Virginia, but no helpful translation emerged. He then went on for two days of meetings with Warren Cooper, National's Foreign Minister, who was, of course, still in office because of the writs. Loyal toasts to America and its great navy were drunk all round and New Zealand's undying adherence to ANZUS was pledged, but Schultz went back to Washington an irritated and suspicious man.

'Jesus H. Christ!' he is said to have exploded when he got back to his office, 'they got a motel proprietor down there who thinks he's Foreign Minister and a stand-up comic they just made Prime Minister! How can you deal with guys like that?'

It was pointed out to him by an aide that President Reagan had once starred in a series of films with Bonzo the Chimpanzee, but was now the leader of the Free World. The aide was assigned to Beirut forthwith.

So within a few days of the election the major themes of the Fourth Labour Government had been established: radical economic reform, ruthlessly pushed through, and conflict with America. It took some time for the public to realise what was happening, as these letters to *The Press* in Christchurch, written in the post-election week, demonstrate:

Dear Sir,
What on earth is all this fuss about American ships being nuclear-armed and powered? I

was in the Home Guard in Wellington in 1942, when the Marines arrived, and I can tell you I was damned glad to see them. It would never have occurred to anybody to ask them if they were nuclear-powered: that would have been an act of gross discourtesy to visitors to our shores. Some of their ships probably *were* nuclear-powered; certainly I never saw any of them taking on coal. But as they sailed off to Japan, leaving thousands of nylon-clad, pregnant women behind them, the last thing we were concerned about was their mode of propulsion. I say to David Lange – wake up and smell the roses! I don't know what that means, but I heard it on television the other night.

Yours etc,

ONE WHO KNOWS ON WHICH SIDE HIS BREAD IS BUTTERED

And another reader wrote:

Dear Sir,

At last we have elected a caring, sharing government which will undo the damage done by the naked, unregulated capitalism of the Muldoon years. A government which will protect the weak against the strong and the poor against the rich: a government which believes that all men are created equal and should remain so. A government which will bring us together, bind our wounds, and dry our tears. David and Roger, once more across the rolling waters of the South Pacific, let the socialist beacon blaze forth!

Yours etc,

RAILWAY WORKER

Other concerns agitated other minds:

Dear Sir,

I put out my rubbish at 9.10am precisely, as I always do. But the truck came by at 9.05am, when I was on the toilet. How much longer do we have to put up with this sort of thing?

Yours etc,

ANGRY RATEPAYER

All these matters were shortly to be addressed.

Chapter Three

1985, The Year of the French
(and the Americans, the 'Boks
and the Students of Oxford)

Some years are more eventful than others, and some are less so. For students of these matters it is interesting to note that the numbers 1-9-8-5, added together, amount to 23. And 2 plus 3 equals 5, which is the last digit in 1985. Conversely, if you subtract 1 from 9, you are left with 8, and if you then take the remaining 8 away from 1985 you are again left with 5. This cannot be mere coincidence and should have alerted all New Zealanders to the nature of the year they were about to face.

There were five major crises or excitements (depending on your point of view) during this dramatic year. They were:

1. The cancellation of the visit of the American warship, *Charles F. Buchanan*, because the US Government would not tell us whether or not it was nuclear-armed.
2. David Lange's triumph in the Oxford Union debate (linked to 1 above).
3. The blowing-up by the French of the *Rainbow Warrior* at Marsden Wharf in Auckland harbour (linked to 1 above in that both involved the presence of weapons in our harbours).
4. The court-ordered cancellation of the All Black tour to South Africa. This was a judicial rather than a maritime detonation, but resulted in the proposed tour ending not with a bang but a whimper, from the New Zealand Rugby Football Union.
5. Keri Hulme's *the bone people* won the 1985 Booker Prize.

Let us deal with this last event first. It was not much of a consolation to rugby players for the loss of the tour but one could, to adopt a rugby idiom, convincingly proclaim that New Zealand literature was the winner. Paul Theroux, one of the Booker judges, was rude about *the bone people*, but as he was later to go on and criticise the eating habits of the much-loved Dame Cath Tizard, at the time our Governor-General, his opinions can be discounted as those of a man determined to blacken New Zealand's name at every opportunity.

A complex, disturbing work, many years in the writing, *the bone people* divided opinion between those who found it utterly unreadable, and those who found it utterly compelling. A decade later it remains a monumental presence in our literature, as does its author, notable for her ability to sustain herself by whitebaiting as well as by novel-writing. One of the present writer's proudest boasts is that he owns a sofa which has been slept on by Keri Hulme and Tony Fomison, though not both at the same time.

The Balance of Error

American armed forces have fought their country's battles from the halls of Montezuma to the shores of Tripoli. But in 1985 it turned out that Auckland was off-limits. The US Navy, testing our anti-nuclear stance, proposed to send a vessel, the *Charles F. Buchanan* (whoever *he* was), on a visit to New Zealand. Much confusion resulted, especially as the Prime Minister, David Lange, was out of the country at the time. The government appeared to be divided between those who didn't know what was happening, and those who did know what was happening but didn't know what to do about it. The Americans compounded the confusion by refusing to confirm or deny that the ship was nuclear-armed or powered. They would confirm that there were Coca-Cola dispensers on board, but that was as far as they would go. Lange eventually seized the helm, as it were, and barred the ship's entry into our waters. This caused public fury in Washington and private fury in Canberra, but much elation throughout New Zealand, except among the defence establishment and the sex industry, whose interests often march hand in hand. The National Party Opposition purported to be outraged, but was in a cleft stick, since the sight of a small nation standing up to a big, bullying one actually appealed to a substantial number of National supporters, many of whom were not keen on nuclear weapons themselves. ANZUS, of course, collapsed, but the Second World War seemed a long way away, in an age in which everyone drove Japanese cars and owned Japanese VCRs. And the Cold War was palpably cooling: within not much more than a year President Reagan and Chairman Gorbachev, at Reykjavik, came within 36 centimetres of abolishing nuclear weapons altogether.

None of this was known in 1985, of course, which enabled David Lange to score New Zealand's biggest foreign policy triumph since its participation in the founding of the United Nations in 1945.

This occurred during:

The Oxford Union Debate

Lange's success during the Oxford Union debate was the major achievement of the Fourth Labour Government. Before we turn to the event itself, let us pause to take stock of the man who for a few golden hours bestrode the narrow world like a colossus – which he had once been. When Lange entered Parliament in 1977 he had black hair, black horn-rimmed glasses and wore black suits. He was also enormously fat; fatter even than Norman Kirk had been before the image-makers got to work on him. The difference was that

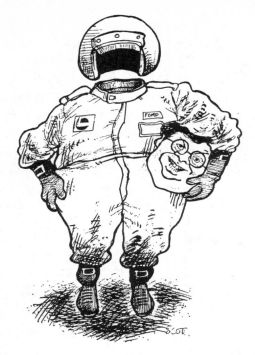

The Prime Minister takes up a dangerous hobby

Lange survived the refurbishing process, whereas Kirk didn't. By the time of the Oxford Union debate, Lange no longer resembled a sumo wrestler in a suit. He had lost weight, wore stylish spectacles and his hair was attractively coiffured. His booming voice had not altered and his jokes were probably no better than they had ever been, but they somehow seemed sharper, coming as they did from a Prime Minister, rather than the juvenile Falstaff who had become leader of the Labour Party by the simple expedient of placing the bird-like figure of Bill Rowling on the sofa of the Labour Party and then sitting on him. In many ways, in the early eighties, the party president, Jim Anderton, was more represent-ative of the rank and file than Lange, but it was Lange who had the one-liners, Lange who led the party in debates in Parliament, and Lange who was good on television. These three attributes coalesced during his apotheosis in the Oxford Union debate. The writer and the illustrator of this book watched the debate at the home of the illustrator and both, misty-eyed, remarked that at last we had a Prime Minister we could send abroad without shame.

Disillusion was to set in, as it always does, but at the time Lange's performance seemed remarkable. Addressed to a demented young student, his line 'I can smell the uranium on your breath' was a fine impromptu, and certainly one unlikely to have been delivered by Muldoon, Rowling, Kirk, Marshall, Holyoake, Nash, Holland, Fraser, Savage, Forbes, Coates, Ward, Massey or Seddon, to name but fourteen of his predecessors. Lange was lucky in that his principal opponent in the debate was the Reverend Jerry Falwell.

Falwell was a Bible-belt fundamentalist, who clearly looked forward to a nuclear holocaust as a means of cleansing the planet, and confronted Lange's wit with the Word of God. This was a tactical mistake, as God is not noted for His wit. His rhetorical powers are impressive, as evidenced by His thunderings in the Old Testament, but He is not seen to His best advantage in debate; indeed He gives the distinct impression that He does not approve of debate. So Falwell was handicapped from the start, and Lange was free, like a trumpeting elephant, to roam the savannahs of the debate, squashing his opponents' huts and flattening their crops. It was an impressive and enjoyable sight. If only history could have been frozen at that moment. But it always moves on – and in the Elysée Palace, and in the undersea naval academies of Corsica, plans were being laid...

Aux Armes, Mes Saboteurs! Formez Vos Zodiacs!

After the Second World War, relations between New Zealand and France were more or less non-existent, until France began testing nuclear bombs in the atmosphere at Moruroa in the late sixties. New Zealand led the opposition to this practice and in 1972 sent a frigate into the test zone with a brave but expendable Cabinet Minister on board to symbolise its opposition. France went underground, but the protests continued, the role of the Royal New Zealand Navy being taken over by an organisation called Greenpeas (Greenpeace is a misspelling). Greenpeas was able to step into the protest vacuum because the supply of New Zealand Cabinet Ministers willing to risk irradiation had dried up, and because Greenpeas was extraordinarily good at manipulating the media, especially in New Zealand. Its spokespeople made no pretence of objectivity when being interviewed, but that was fair enough, they didn't have to. The problem was, the journalists interviewing them made no pretence of objectivity either, and this did matter, because it meant the validity, legality or ordinary common sense of Greenpeas's actions were subject to no scrutiny whatsoever. Greenpeas howled 'Illegality!' whenever it encountered opposition by any authority it was attacking, but its own activities depended on their illegality for the media-appeal which was the life-blood of the organisation.

Be that as it may, Greenpeas certainly put the wind up the French when they proposed in 1985 to sail a vessel called *Rainbow Warrior* into the exclusion zone around the Moruroa test site. The French Defence Minister, and his Prime Minister, and, one may fairly assume, President Mitterrand himself, decided that the security of France was threatened by this action. Goodness knows what they were drinking at the time: Napoleon brandy, one concludes, since they appear to have assumed that they were the spiritual and military heirs of the little Corsican.

The Secret Service was entrusted with the mission of destroying the *Rainbow Warrior*; (what a silly name, by the way, may as well call the vessel *Aurora Condottiere*, or *Half-Moon Halberdier*, or even *Tequila Sunrise*). The *Warrior* was due to dock at Auckland in June 1985, and so the sparkling waters of the Waitemata were chosen as the venue for the daring exploit which would prove to the world that France was not to be trifled with.

Well, the French proved that all right. The ship was sunk at Marsden Wharf, but a crewman was drowned. This deprived France of the moral victory it would otherwise have claimed, but France suffered no other penalty. Two saboteurs were captured, while the others all went skiing. The captured pair were put on trial, pleaded guilty to manslaughter and were sentenced to ten years' imprisonment. But New Zealand found itself completely isolated. The British and the Americans, no doubt because we had told their ships to bugger off, maintained a studied silence and refused to condemn an act of piracy and terrorism committed in the waters of a country which had spilled its blood and treasure for them in two world wars. And the French were left free to exert such commercial pressure against New Zealand that the agents were eventually sprung from durance vile in our own prisons and sent to 'captivity' in a French possession, the Pacific island of Hao, whence, to no one's surprise, they were soon repatriated to France on medical grounds. A narrative poem that the present writer published at the time conveys something of the flavour of events.

The David
after Edgar Allan Poe

Once upon a midnight dreary, limpet mines exploded clearly,
And a Greenpeace vessel settled on the muddy harbour floor.
Soon 'twas clear that Frenchmen did it, though from Mitterrand they hid it:
But for France they tried to rid it, of a threat they thought they saw;
Of a threat to nuclear testing which the DGSE saw,
Which *la France* could not ignore.

Soon the agents were arrested, and New Zealand courts were tested,
But Alain and Dominique were duly sentenced under law,
And 'twas then that people started asking David, lionhearted,
'Could the criminals be bartered for some butter sales offshore?'
Quoth the David, 'Nevermore.'

Many times the David said it, many times the people read it,
Bold assertions none need edit, all delivered in a roar.
'Yes we have them and we'll hold them; who would dare suggest we sold them?'
'Quite, but could you not parole them, so the French would not be sore?'
Quoth the David, 'Nevermore.'

'But then what about our butter? Pray, what comfort can you utter
To our stricken dairy farmers if the Frenchmen close the door?

Though the EEC you're wooing, it is us the Frogs are screwing,
And we'll all be facing ruin in defence of common law.
Is there no way you could find a little loophole in the law?'
Quoth the David, 'Nevermore'.

Then the ante grew much higher and they called in P. de Cuellar,
So that we could sell our principles but not appear a whore.
'He's a brilliant arbitrator,' David boomed, 'there's none who's greater.
He'll unhook us now or later, that is what he's in there for.'
'Does this mean you'll spring the agents and avoid a butter war?
Buy us time to sell our butter for a precious few months more?'
Quoth the David, 'Oh, all right then.'

Rugby was the Loser

The South African Rugby Union invited an All Black side to tour the Republic in 1985. This caused great agitation, especially among those who had marched in '81 and now saw, with sinking hearts, that they might be called upon to march again. Many conflicting points of principle were involved. There is no doubt that the government would have refused a Springbok team admission to New Zealand, but this time our boys were going over there, and it is a serious matter to deny New Zealanders the right to depart from their own shores: there is no distinction in international or constitutional law between young New Zealanders wanting to play rugby in South Africa and more senior ones wishing to have holidays in Surfers or Fiji. The government appeared helpless and the New Zealand Rugby Union maintained that it was powerless to prevent itself from sending a team to the Republic. All seemed set for a very messy winter; police fingers tightened around their long batons while protesters cleaned the bloodstains of '81 off their crash helmets. Then two brilliant young Auckland lawyers, Philip Recordon and Paddy Finnigan, piloted by another brilliant Auckland lawyer, Ted Thomas, brought an action against the Rugby Union, claiming that the proposed tour was against the aims and interests of the union's incorporating document. This was in the days when Auckland lawyers still had principles and were not solely concerned with cooking up (geddit? 'Cooking up') Rarotongan tax transactions. To the nation's surprise, the Court of Appeal ruled that Recordon and Finnigan, as rugby players, had *'locus standi'* (a legal term meaning a place in the grandstand; 'grandstand' itself being an archaic term for a row of corporate boxes).

Empowered by this ruling, Mr Justice 'Moss' Casey issued an injunction preventing the All Blacks from departing to hurl themselves like Polish cavalry against the Springbok panzers. The nation uttered a gasp of disbelief, followed by an even greater gasp of relief, and everybody was happy except the Rugby Union, who had understandably believed up till then that the long arm of the law did not extend over the sideline. Candles burned in front of wayside shrines containing images of Casey, a Catholic, though there were dark mutterings in certain Marist clubrooms. But the injunction was a harbinger of ever-greater judicial intervention in the nation's public affairs, as we shall see when we come to consider Treaty of Waitangi issues. In the meantime the Rugby Union consoled itself by turning a blind eye while a rebel All Black team went to South Africa under the name of the Cavaliers. An unfortunate choice, since Cavaliers, despite their romantic image, usually lose their battles, as proved to be the case on this occasion.

So, did the nation emerge purified, its steel tempered, by the fires of 1985? Was it invigorated and rejuvenated, or eviscerated and discombobulated? What sort of country was New Zealand in '86, '87 and beyond? It is to these questions that we must address ourselves in the chapter which lies ahead.

IF IT WEREN'T FOR THE FACT,
I SUFFER FROM VERTIGO, I'D
GO FOR THE HIGH MORAL GROUND
EVERYTIME

Chapter Four

1986 – 1987:
La Belle Époque

S o what sort of society was it that was undergoing such profound political upheaval, both domestically and on the world stage? What kind of nation could produce Muldoon, Lange and Keri Hulme in such quick succession? What of life, letters, leisure, lager and Limbs? Let us first deal with the last (to use another 'L' word). The success of the Limbs dance company appeared inexplicable to the Terpsichoreanly-challenged, even those with a healthy appreciation of firm young breasts and naked buttocks. The tales told by the lithe and energetic young dancers of Limbs were mostly accompanied by music that sounded like a recording of activities in a panelbeating firm that was not particularly busy. The lighting was either blinding, or green, or more or less non-existent. But the bodies were beautiful, even if the uses to which they were put were sometimes puzzling to the non-*cognoscenti*. And Limbs was new, fashionable and created an audience for later work by Douglas Wright and Michael Parmenter. In the words of Allen Curnow, they were '… something different, something nobody counted on'.

New Zealand painting was in a healthy state in the mid-eighties, with fine work being produced by Ralph Hotere, Michael Smither and Trevor Moffitt, to name but three. Prints were in demand, as were elaborate woollen wall-hangings, of such complexity of structure and vividness of hue that one stood dumb before them, unable either to tear the eye away from them or think of anything to say about them. Potters flourished in these years because everybody gave everyone else pottery for Christmas, and often for birthdays as well. In most New Zealand households, apart from the most disadvantaged, a pottery teapot languishes in a cupboard, unused since 1988, alongside an eclectic selection of pottery coffee mugs that have not contained coffee since 1990.

Such cupboards also contain shapely wine goblets, which lead us, by a natural transition, to the subject of the New Zealand wine industry. We had always had a wine industry, but most of what was produced, from regions such as Henderson and Gisborne, was for domestic consumption. We drank local whites, but most of us preferred Australian reds (and indeed Australian whites, if the truth be told). But in the mid-eighties the suitability of Marlborough for the production of sauvignon blanc, and later of chardonnay, revolutionised New Zealand wine-making. Fine sauvignon blancs and chardonnays started emerging all over the place, not just from Marlborough, and we all became very knowledgeable about them. In the days before the '87 crash, no long lunch was complete without extended demonstrations of connoisseurship – entirely justified, because the wines were receiving recognition around the world and actually winning prizes. Much to the fury of the French; and it is probably no coincidence that the aforementioned *Rainbow Warrior* was attacked in our waters by French saboteurs at about the same time as our sauvignon blanc started to capture an increasing share of the British dry white market. There is no actual evidence for this supposition, but then if all suppositions had to be founded on evidence, the writing of history would be a very dull affair indeed.

A curious phenomenon which became popular round about the same time as stylish wine-making was deer farming – or rather, investing in the same – and goat farming, which also attracted the disposable capital of surgeons, entertainers, and some classes of people even more dodgy than either of the above. Some of the pre-crash income was also soaked up by salmon, stud horses, empty high-rise office buildings and very bad films. Presumably all this money had to go somewhere, but at least with high-rise office buildings and very bad films you got something for your money, whereas deer and goats were for us the equivalent in the eighties of the Dutch craze for tulip bulbs in the early eighteenth century. In fact it is a pity we didn't have a tulip bulb craze going at the same time, so that when it all fell apart the tulip bulbs could have been fed to the deer and goats, and a very bad film made about the suicide of an Auckland surgeon who had invested in all four.

What about poetry, does one hear the cry? What of the principal glory of the English language – and, of course, guaranteed by the Treaty partnership – the principal glory of the Maori language as well? It wasn't a bad time for poets: Kevin Ireland had returned from England, Anne French was hitting the straps, Louis Johnson was still practising, young poets were like rockets bursting over a concert in the Auckland Domain, and Sam Hunt was at the peak of his fame, eclipsing even the renown of his friend and colleague Gary McCormick, who was later to become so famous that the only New Zealand television programme on which he has never appeared on is the section of One Network News devoted to tomorrow's weather.

Which by another deft and subtle transition leads us on to a consideration of the state of television in the mid-eighties. Modesty forbids your historian from dwelling on the success of a programme called *McPhail & Gadsby* which he co-wrote with McPhail and Gadsby themselves, but mention should be made of other phenomena, such as the sitcom *Gliding On*, written by Roger Hall and depicting a Public Service that, thanks to Roger Douglas and Richard Prebble, was disappearing into history even as the episodes went to air. Then there was the considerable and deserved success of Billy T. James, a Maori comedian with a personality to which the whole nation warmed, and who was therefore able to make quite rude, non-politically correct jokes about Maori that could not have been made by either (a) a pakeha, or (b) a Maori without Billy's infectious giggle. Alas, because of a heart condition, he was not destined to survive far into the nineties, and was subject to the final indignity of a squalid dispute over the disposal of his remains. On the other hand, perhaps it is particularly appropriate that comedians should be subjected to undignified episodes on the occasion of their passing, given that human indignity is the foundation and essence of so much of their material.

Another home-grown television phenomenon of this era was the programme *Gloss*. Nominally about a fashion magazine, it was mainly about Ilona Rogers in a large red hat saying bitchy things to a sulky Simon Prast. It never attracted a very large audience, but everybody talked about it and wrote about it, which was just as satisfactory from the point of view of the programme makers. And Judy Bailey and Richard Long erected a Dalkon Shield around TV One's Network News, rendering it impervious to the wriggly sperm of TV3.

Community theatres, such as Mercury, Downstage and the Court, flourished during this period, often rescued from impending collapse by a new Roger Hall comedy, which put bums on seats, the bumholders laughing too often to notice that the seats were not very comfortable. You could even get a glass of cask wine at a theatre bar if you were very quick. Such sophistication! Regional opera and national ballet struggled along, under-resourced, under-produced and often under-performed. The New Zealand Symphony Orchestra performed splendidly if (outside Wellington) rarely; it had not yet succumbed to the combination of bickering and bankruptcy that brought it to the brink in the mid-nineties.

The print media, do I hear you cry? What of them? Not a lot happened, apart from the demise of the *Auckland Star* and the rise and demise of the *Auckland Sun*. Perhaps if they had called it the *Auckland Gaseous Mass* it might have had a different fate. Who can say? The most interesting event in the print media occurred in the world of magazines. *Metro*, started up in the early eighties by Warwick Roger, a brilliant editor, as a magazine for Auckland, soon acquired a national readership – partly because many of its articles, although immensely long, were of general interest. People in Wellington, Christchurch or Invercargill bought it to read, in the irreverent 'Felicity Ferret' gossip column, about the doings of Auckland socialites they had never heard of, or whose nicknames they could not penetrate. They did so because the column was funny and saucy.

And also satirical: it cast a sour eye on the goings-on of people whose consumption was not only conspicuous but often crass. New Zealanders aren't very good at flaunting it: they try, but their knickers or trousers either fall down, or are pulled down, in mid-flaunt. They are good at making loud noises in restaurants and rear-ending each other's BMWs. But there is more to style than that. Style was conspicuously absent, too, in the buildings erected in downtown Auckland and Wellington during the property boom of '86 and '87. Hideous when erected, they are even more hideous ten years later, when they have lost the charm of novelty and will fortunately fall down long before they qualify as historic places.

Consumption was most conspicuous in Auckland, where it was naked and unashamed. In Wellington it was naked but slightly ashamed; in Christchurch it was unashamed but fully clothed, and in Dunedin it took place behind closed doors. But there was lots of it

going on: this had much to do with the fact that most New Zealanders, unaccustomed to a boom economy, believed that the double helix of supply and demand would spiral upwards forever: a helical Stairway to Heaven. Historians such as Stevan Eldred-Grigg have pointed out that we have always had very rich people in our society who often made displays of their wealth. But there weren't many of them, and they were mostly displaying their wealth to each other, or in far-off cities like London. The boom of the mid-eighties was the first time when large numbers of New Zealanders felt themselves to be wealthy and wanted to demonstrate it by the public acquisition of desirable objects, such as cars and new wives or husbands.

The compulsory division provisions of the Matrimonial Property Act kept all this new money circulating in a satisfactory way; our tax laws were far from rigidly enforced and, as it seemed at the time, easily circumvented; laws imposing ethical behaviour on companies and traders in their shares were laughable or non-existent; you only had to pick up the phone to borrow money to roll over the loan you had taken out to buy an asset already mortgaged to the hilt – even better, you could raise this money offshore. Why should this party ever end?

Well, it did. After the ball before Waterloo comes Waterloo. And if you are a small country with the most open economy in the developed world, you are abnormally susceptible to developments. In October 1987 Wall Street farted, and the anal sphincter of our economy collapsed, with cloacal results.

Chapter Five

The Dance of Death:
or Labour Goes Doolally

The election of 1987 was won by Labour with an increased share of the vote. This was not because the electorate, especially the traditional Labour section of it, was satisfied with Labour policies: it was because in the winter of 1987 the All Blacks won the first Rugby World Cup. When David Kirk held the World Cup aloft he was also lifting Labour in the line-out. Plus the boom was roaring along, overheating the economy like one of those big cylindrical heaters you see in bottle stores in winter. But in October 1987 someone pulled the plug out. One billion dollars was wiped off the value of the sharemarket in a day. Where could

it have gone? Was it ever there in the first place? How could it just disappear? Could one work the same trick with one's overdraft? No one knew the answers – least of all the free-marketeers. All they knew was that the shares they had borrowed to buy were now worthless, and so were the BMWs they had borrowed to buy, since the *Herald* was listing 800 BMWs for sale every Saturday morning. It was just awful! Houses were sold; on the other hand many married couples stayed together because there was no longer any matrimonial property to divide. Companies collapsed and banks discovered that they had over-exposed their private parts to borrowers who had over-exposed *their* private parts to other banks.

Into this chaos stepped Roger Douglas, with his proposal of a flat tax, 20 per cent for all, rich or poor. Obviously the richer you were the better this deal was, because although you were paying more tax in actual dollars and cents than a poor person, you had many more dollars and cents left over afterwards. Cabinet agreed to this proposal in December 1987, but in January 1988 David Lange began to brood. Brooding led, uncharacteristically, to unilateral action. Lange squashed the flat tax flat while Douglas was overseas. It was time, Lange said, for a cup of tea.

Douglas was furious. There was a certain irony to this, since he, Douglas, had been behaving unilaterally since 1984, but behaved like a five-year-old who had eaten too much chocolate at a birthday party, when somebody else did the same.

Anyway, he flew home to resurrect his scheme, but no amount of whiteboard explanations of its wonders availed him. His clever plan drowned in an ocean of tea. He never forgave Lange: he came to see Lange as a rather large pimple on the otherwise unblemished forehead of Rogernomics. Short men never like big men, and Douglas decided it was time for this big man to get out of the sunlight. Bees in Beehive bonnets began buzzing.

SOE, or Sell Off Everything

The SOE was largely the brainchild of Dr Roderick Deane, who later became the head of a privatised SOE, Telecom, at an annual salary of more than $1,000,000. Few public servants have been able to convert their fantasies into reality on quite such a rewarding scale. The basic idea of the SOE, like all great ideas, e.g. relativity, was both simple and hard to grasp. You took a government department, like the New Zealand Electricity Department, turned it into a company with a new name like Electricorp, and endowed it with a huge paper loan from the government, so it could buy itself from the government, which was its sole shareholder.

Why had nobody thought of this before? Presumably because most New Zealanders were comfortable with the idea of their government owning institutions and conducting activities which were important in their lives, like the supply of electricity, or the holding of their pensions, or the delivery of their letters, or conveying them round the country in aeroplanes. Comfortable with this state of affairs New Zealanders may have been, but in the view of Deane and Douglas and his mullahs of the Treasury, the time for comfort was past. It was time for the kindly, paternal face of the State to assume a scowl and complain to its children that it wasn't made of money: the kids should get out of the house, get a job and accept that they were going to be cut out of the will.

This came as something of a shock to the New Zealanders who had re-elected the Labour Government, little realising that it was going to take their post offices away from them. The local post office had always represented the benign face of the State, and, what is more, it was convenient because there were plenty of them: somewhat run-down, but you could pay the phone bill, post your letters and conduct banking transactions just as important to you as the mercantile transactions of Fay and Richwhite were to them.

Well, the post offices went anyway. Empty ones were converted into restaurants or massage parlours (perhaps a slight exaggeration), while the vestigial remnants sold everything from cellphones and ghastly postcards to hamburgers (another exaggeration, but not by much). The Post Office Savings Bank was sold to the ANZ Bank and renamed 'Postbank' though why they bothered to keep the name 'Post' in the title is a puzzle, since you couldn't buy stamps there, or, for that matter, postcards or hamburgers. The People's Bank was just another bank and the ancient New Zealand practice of opening a POSB account for a newborn grandchild fell into desuetude. Richard Prebble defended the abolition of post offices on the grounds of efficiency: a classic example of a politician out of touch with the warp and woof of the lives of the people his party claimed to represent.

He was to pay for this eventually, but by the time he did, the cosy and comforting constellation of post offices had vanished into the black hole of Treasury theory.

The Treasury! Dum-de-dah-dah-dah!

This is an appropriate point to consider the malign role of the Treasury in New Zealand affairs. Staffed almost entirely, it would seem, by ideologues from the University of Canterbury School of Economics, themselves taught by lecturers who masturbated to images of Milton Friedman, it chafed impotently under the iron hand of Muldoon, and then, like Frankenstein's monster, burst from its bonds in 1984 and began striding about the landscape, terrifying peasants and every Cabinet Minister who wasn't Roger Douglas. Was Douglas the creature of the Creature, or did he, as he claimed, have it under control? It doesn't much matter; every mad idea that Treasury came up with was eventually translated into legislation by Douglas, Richardson or Birch. (I exempt Caygill from this line-up of Finance Ministers because he wasn't there for long enough to do much more than sign letters dictated by Treasury. On the other hand it was Caygill who introduced the infamous Reserve Bank Act, which committed the Governor of the Bank, on terms of loss of his job, to hold inflation at between zero and two per cent. More of that later. This parenthesis has gone on for long enough already.)

The problem with Treasury, during the years under review, was that it didn't just advise the government; it *was* the government. Jim Hacker, in *Yes, Minister*, put up a feeble show of resistance from time to time: a New Zealand version of that programme would have had to be called *Yes, Secretary*, with Ministers bowing and scraping and offering human sacrifices before whichever Moloch happened to be Secretary of the Treasury at the time. An unedifying spectacle: tribunes of the people delivering themselves bound hand and foot to the one department that would never be privatised because it was busy privatising all the others.

Treasury is supposed to advise and warn governments, not order them about. But the mujahadeen of Treasury believed they were divinely inspired, and they imposed an orthodoxy faithfully conveyed to the public by successive governments and the press. If you opposed it, the stake and the faggots were waiting. Economic heresies, such as 'Hang on, maybe there's another side to this and another way of ordering society', could not be allowed to threaten the theology of Treasury or the interests of the Business Roundtable, a gathering distinctly less than chivalric, which would have given the noble and saintly King Arthur a stomach ulcer.

The Deconstruction of Politics

While all this restructuring was going on, the Labour Cabinet was deconstructing itself. During 1988 Douglas, with the aid of an able press secretary, Bevan Burgess, set about destabilising the man whose popular appeal had put Douglas in a position from which he could ram through policies which would destroy Labour's popularity for years to

come. The Beehive became a battleground, with explosive press releases flying round corridors like Cruise missiles seeking their target. The Cabinet was coming unglued and much dirty linen was spilling out of it. But there was no paralysis: the assets sales programme continued apace. Air New Zealand, BNZ, Railways, Telecom, Government Print, the Rural Bank, all were sold. New corps kept popping up: Forestcorp, Landcorp, Coalcorp.

Lange, who was a sort of Corpcorp (short for Corpulent Corporation), introduced Tomorrow's Schools, a radical scheme invented by a supermarket proprietor who happened to be a friend of Lange. The Education Department and local education boards were abolished. An emaciated Ministry of Education replaced them, and control of individual schools was handed over to boards of trustees, elected from the ranks of parents, with the principal of a school as the board's CEO. This was a rotten idea: boards were soon at odds with their principals and principals with their staff. And the unfortunate parents who were elected to boards found themselves doing for a pittance work that had previously been done by salaried professionals. Democracy is all very well, but you can't run an army or a hospital operating theatre that way. Nor a supermarket if it comes to that: you may have choice within it but not about what you pay at the checkout. A State school system should be run by the State; otherwise all sorts of inequities arise between schools in wealthy middle-class areas, with adequately resourced parents as a cushion, and schools in industrial or rural areas. Education should be spread evenly like Marmite, but that costs money. The democratic ingredient should be that schools are administered by a democratically elected government, not by amateur educationists.

The Unholy Trinity: Lange, Palmer and Moore

While all this creative ferment was going on, marsh gases were being emitted from the swamp of Labour politics. The relationship between Lange and his Finance Minister was like the elastic in a pair of over-laundered knickers; it had been strained too often and no longer served any useful purpose. Lange sacked Douglas. It was a hollow victory. Under Labour rules caucus was entitled to re-elect Douglas to the Cabinet and in due course it did so. Lange declared that working with Douglas was like a 'living death' and sacked himself, though not before he had sacked Richard Prebble, a Rogernome who had questioned Lange's emotional stability. A bit rough, really; if Lange was, in Prebble's eyes, a bit of a flake, Prebble was, in most people's eyes, a Mexican jumping bean with teeth.

Anyway, Lange departed and handed over the reins of power to Geoffrey Palmer. Palmer was a legal academic from Victoria University, who spoke in a very loud voice, ringing with certitude, and conveying the impression that he was spelling things out to you very clearly because you would otherwise be too stupid to understand them. This style may have worked with Victoria law students, but the electorate didn't like it, a fact which became increasingly apparent as the 1990 election loomed. The history of the last six years did not come back to haunt Labour; the party was still drowning in the middle of it, and in desperation Labour invited Geoffrey to fall upon his sword. This he did with some dignity: nothing in his premiership so became him as the leaving of it, and he departed from one corn-producing area, Parliament, to thunder in the middle of another at the University of Iowa.

Six weeks out from the election, Geoff was replaced by Mike Moore, with Helen Clark as his deputy. This could have been a dream team, if they had had more time to evoke dreams and expunge Labour supporters' waking nightmares. Moore, a popular populist (not a tautology because the sands of history are littered with the bones of unpopular populists), was, like Prebble, a Mexican jumping bean but one whom people liked because he had the gift of the gab they spoke themselves and was somehow, as Trade Minister, off to one side of what the rest of his party had been up to since 1984.

Helen Clark, yet another of the academics which Labour, party of working men and the underprivileged, seems obsessed with promoting into the top jobs (Palmer, Clark, and, more recently, Cullen and Maharey), was not a Mexican jumping bean. She was more like a stick of celery. As it turned out, she was more like a sharpened stick of bamboo, but that is for a later chapter. Moore and Clark were, on the far side of the yawning chasm of the 1990 election, to prove an effective combination. But, as this chapter concludes, they were marching confidently towards a crevasse that they knew was waiting for them and which had their number on it.

Chapter Six

Waitangi;
or Sad, Muddy Waters

Before turning to the electoral belch of 1990 it is appropriate to consider here the eruption of Maori grievances, land and fishing claims, which began in the years 1985-90, and which, by 1995, would teach the pakeha majority that a Maori occupation was something more than driving a bulldozer while playing the guitar. To gain historical perspective we need to go back to the Treaty of Waitangi. Now claimed by both the Crown and Maori to be our founding document, it was in fact a hastily compiled, loosely worded 'work on paper', as printmakers would say, misunderstood by all the parties to it and never signed by many of the iwi to whom it applied. It purported to give Queen Wikitoria sovereignty over New Zealand while at the same time guaranteeing Maori sovereignty over the same islands, particularly with regard to land and fishing rights; and, as claimed by Maori in the 1990s, over the World, the Universe, Space. White settlement proceeded apace after its signature, and, as observed in our earlier work, *The Paua and the Glory*, it set the scene for a conflict in which both Maori and pakeha wanted the same thing: Maori land.

In the nineteenth century this conflict was resolved in favour of pakeha, thanks to shonky, unhonoured deals and military force; any land not dealt to by these means was scooped up by the handy, imposed instrument of the Native Land Courts.

For most of our island story the Treaty was perceived by Maori to be a fraud, but in the 1970s and 1980s a class of intelligent, dynamic and angry Maori realised that this fraud could be turned back upon its perpetrator. The pebble which started the avalanche was probably a decision of the late Mr Justice Williamson in 1985, in which he held that the Treaty guaranteed Maori certain rights over harvesting of the fruits of the sea. By then the Waitangi Tribunal was in existence, originally established only to deal with Maori grievances arising after 1975. But the Labour Government, in its well-meaning but feckless way, decided to extend the Tribunal's jurisdiction to any grievances arising after 6 February 1840, the date of the signing of the Treaty. Maori suddenly found themselves pushing on an open door, and choruses of 'Ten Guitars' drowned the nation in song.

The Tribunal was given jurisdiction to make findings in respect of Crown land only, not private freehold land. And its findings were to be advisory to and not binding

upon the government. So what! Most of the South Island was Crown land of one sort or another. And it was soon discovered by Maori scholars that coastal tribes had been operating a 200-mile economic fishing zone for centuries before the arrival of the pakeha, using deep-sea trawlers with flaxen sails, and onshore stations processing the catch into cans made of yet more flax. And tino rangatiratanga meant that Maori were conscious of their sovereignty over the airwaves long before any waves were actually rippling through the air.

The long brown arm of the Treaty acquired fresh muscle when Labour incorporated into the act setting up its SOEs a provision requiring them to have regard to the principles of the Treaty. This empowered Baron Cooke of Thorndon, as he later became, to enable the Court of Appeal to surf along the banzai pipeline of Maori claims. Suddenly the pakeha majority was being forced to look into its nappies and find them soiled. To its credit, the government (by then National) decided to deal honourably with these matters and appointed an able and articulate Minister, Doug Graham, to attend to them. He concluded the 'Sealord' deal, which gave Maori substantial interests in fishing. The problem was that there was nothing in the deal for non-coastal tribes, and that matter has still to be resolved. Your present historian urged, through the columns of the *Listener*, a simpler solution, but it was totally ignored, to the nation's cost. The Grant proposal was that the Treaty guarantees should apply (a) only to fish alive at the time of the signing of the

Treaty; (b) to fish descended from fish alive at the time of the signing of the Treaty; (c) to fish fluent in the taonga of the Maori language. But did the government listen to this sage advice? It did not. Instead it put Sir Tipene O'Regan in charge of a commission perceived by urban, deracinated Maori, and by non-coastal Maori, to be acting in its own interests. And in respect of land claims the government, in the face of substantial opposition, pressed on with something called 'the fiscal envelope', which sought to put a $1 billion cap on Maori claims. The envelope was not capacious enough to hold all the money that was going to have to be stuffed into it, and is bound to split sooner or later. But this has not happened yet, and in the meantime Tainui have got $170 million out of it, plus a sort of apology from Queen Elizabeth, or Irihapeti the Second. There are those who think the Queen should have been forced to pay the $170 million out of her own fortune. She could afford to, and she *is* the Crown after all.

The pace of restitution was not fast enough for some Maori, who began occupying, for various periods of time, lands under claim before the Tribunal, or sometimes just lands with a nice view of the sea or a river frontage. Such occupations attracted controlled police attention and fantastic media coverage, which was, of course, the point of them. But their flamboyance could not obscure the steady addressing of grievances; a political development greatly to the credit of both Labour and National Governments. One can despair of politicians, but there are times when they surprise one by behaving well. The bipartisan settlement of Maori grievances is a process which, against the dark backdrop

of democracy in the eighties and nineties, flickers, in the words of the children's hymn, 'like a little candle/Shining in the night'.

But it is not all over yet, and a new mood of Maori militancy is signified by the words of a marching song heard increasingly on the marae. (It is sung, accompanied by ten guitars, to the tune of 'Maori Battalion'):

> Maori land claimants, march to victory.
> Maori land claimants, staunch and true.
> Maori land claimants, march to glory.
> The Tribunal is alongside you.
> And we'll scowl, scowl, scowl at the Government.
> With a most ferocious frown,
> Till we gain a glorious settlement
> From Queen Wikitoria's guilty Crown!

Chapter Seven

The Millennium Neareth:
With All That Pertains Thereunto

On 27 October 1990, one of New Zealand's numerous electoral revolutions occurred. Labour was sent hurtling down the hydroslide of politics and sank to the bottom of the pool. National, under Jim Bolger, was returned to power with a majority of thirty-nine seats.

These electoral revolutions had been happening with increasing frequency during the latter years of the century: Labour enjoyed two, in 1972 and 1984; National likewise had two, in 1975 and 1990. Intermediate elections in 1978 and 1981 resulted in a government being returned with a minority of the popular vote. The voting public were either decisive or indecisive, and nobody, least of all the voting public themselves, could

predict what sort of mood they would be in on the day when, behind a piece of scrim, with their trousers or stockings exposed from knee-level down, they picked up the carpenter's pencil and ticked or crossed according to subconscious urgings. But they were undoubtedly decisive on 27 October 1990 and voted for Jim Bolger's 'decent society' and the repeal of the superannuation surcharge.

We will have more to say about Bolger in chapters waiting to be born. But this is a convenient place from which to assess the gumbooted cocky from the King Country. And he deserved to be cocky, having achieved a popular mandate to break promises in all directions. What sort of man was, and is, he? Few can say. Even his wife Joan can only tell us that he gets up, singing, in the morning. Given that she has borne him nine children, Jim's matutinal ebullience is perhaps hardly surprising, but all this happened before he became Prime Minister. To repeat the question, what sort of man was Bolger on the morning of Sunday 29 October 1990? Who looked at Jim Bolger in the bathroom mirror on that triumphal Sunday morning?

A man with a cheery face, a tongue inclined to get in the way of syllable, and a brain inclined to get in the way of thought. A devoted acolyte of Muldoon; a man who adopted, under Rob, principles he would cheerfully disown once he became his own man.

But what sort of 'own man' was he? To keep having to ask the question is to keep having to remind oneself that there is no answer to it.

Who owned the 'own man' that Jim Bolger had become? The answer has to be Bill Birch, the Cardinal Richelieu of New Zealand politics. When Bill jerks the chain, Jim stops growling, unless Bill has ordered him to growl. Quite why Birch should have this eerie power, not only over Jim but over the National Party caucus, is another question never to be answered, least of all by Bill, whose command of language is less than considerable, and whose voice tones betray that fact. If there is a poet imprisoned within Bill, he is not struggling to be let out.

Churchill said of Russia that it is 'a riddle wrapped in a mystery inside an enigma'. A description applicable to both Bill and Jim, except that when one finally unwrapped the riddle one would find oneself confronted by a blank piece of paper. Which is not to say that neither Bill nor Jim are incapable of decisive action. They are like puppets, pulling each other's strings and, when that happens, limbs do jerk into life. The first decisive action they took, very shortly after the election, was to pour $700 million into the BNZ, to save it from collapse. They were close to collapse themselves when they came to power and found that the BNZ had exposed itself in the marketplace and was in danger of arrest. They saved it, so they could later onload it to the National Australia Bank (it should have been renamed 'The National Bank of Australia, New Zealand, and the Ross Dependency, with Emphasis on the Dependent' – a cumbersome title, but an accurate one).

The next decisive action, partly prompted by the first, was to slash welfare benefits. This depressed not only the economy but the recipients of the benefits. It was prompted by the remarkable figure of Ruth Richardson.

If Jim was Eisenhower, and Bill was Field-Marshal Kesselring, Ruth was Rommel. Decisive thrusts in all directions, and she won every battle but the last one, leaving a desert behind her. She believed in the free market, ignoring, like the Treasury mandarins and her Labour predecessors, the fact that when you are in the marketplace trying to buy something like health or education, the marketplace is an extremely expensive place to be. And particularly expensive if all you have is two coins to rub together to keep your fingers warm.

Short and fierce, with a voice like a shovel being scraped over concrete, she was not unattractive, if you like short, fierce women with metallic voices. Like Margaret Thatcher, she was a dominatrix, having learned that masochism is a powerful emotion in politics. People like you to give them stick, even though they don't enjoy it. Not enjoying it is what in fact they *do* enjoy. No gain without pain: pain is the price of sexual arousal. This is not to suggest that anybody was sexually aroused by Ruth, apart from her husband, but power is a heady aphrodisiac, and when people saw or listened to Ruth they lay back and thought of their PT instructor. Especially when she brought forth 'the Mother of All Budgets'. She delivered it on television, wearing a red jacket. She should have had the decency to wear a black armband, since the MoAB sounded the death-knell of free health services and the modest incomes of superannuitants. Grey anger flared, and its flames were to scorch the National Government in 1993.

Nineteen ninety was also the year in which corporal punishment was abolished in

schools. No longer would quivering naked buttocks be exposed to slake the lusts of members of the Post Primary Teachers' Association. Parents, far too cowardly to administer such condign punishment to their own hulking fifteen-year-olds, nevertheless objected to schools refusing to do so. And the parents were right.

Look at the results! Rampant inflation (3.16 per cent by some calculations), Swedish hitchhikers murdered on the Coromandel, the Employment Contracts Act brought into law and the death of Billy T. Is it reasonable to link all these matters to the abolition of corporal punishment in schools? Your author and illustrator think so. What else can they be linked to? Is there a pattern to human existence or is there not? Round these parts, we go for patterns. Fortified, we might add, by the resignation from Parliament of Sir Robert Muldoon.

He could see which way the wind was blowing. Physical chastisement, whether administered by the State or taking place within a caring, sharing domestic environment, was part of the 'I will give them stick' ethos in which the former PM believed. Once it became against the law, there was no point in sticking around. 'No point in no pain,' he growled to himself, and departed, leaving our politics a great deal poorer than he had found them.

A Titan had left our midst, and just as well.

The financial situation in 1990 was serious. On top of the $700 million poured into the BNZ, the stabilisation of the Clyde dam was revealed to cost $337 million, and the legal aid bill for the defence of the couple alleged to have seen off Peter Plumley-Walker, a cricket umpire, no less, amounted to $473,243. As a nation, we were losing money hand over fist. The sale of Telecom was a mere drop of water in the malt whisky of national debt. If not quite bankrupt, we were certainly deeply recessed.

But 'mustn't grumble!'. We had the Commonwealth Games in Auckland, complete with a spectacular if somewhat incomprehensible opening ceremony. New Zealand yachts finished first and second in the Whitbread Round The World Extremely Lengthy Yacht Race. And there was always Auckland rugby. By 1990 Auckland had held the Ranfurly Shield for five years, thanks to Grant Fox's extraordinary breathing techniques, and the invention of the Zinzan Brooke pushover try, the most boring way of scoring a try imaginable, but certainly effective. And there were great players in the Auckland side like John Kirwan, whom Grant Fox sometimes allowed a bit of a run. The problem with Auckland was its coach, John Hart, brilliant in the role but determined to unseat Alex Wyllie, the incumbent coach, whose side had won the 1987 World Cup. Hart was grafted on to Wyllie for the 1991 competition: the graft did not take and the All Blacks relinquished the Cup to Australia.

Wyllie departed gruffly for South Africa, and his successor was not Hart, making a nonsense of the 'graft', but Otago's Laurie Mains, a man with the peculiar habit of not looking at anybody who was talking to him. Laurie had a chequered career as All Black coach and was eventually to lose the 1995 World Cup, which we should have won. The

1990s were a bad era for New Zealand sport as far as World Cups were concerned: we lost the 1991 and 1995 Rugby World Cups, as well as the 1992 Cricket World Cup, playing brilliantly all the way to the semi-finals and then inexplicably crashing to defeat against Imran Khan's Pakistan side. Perhaps our team was undermined by the knowledge that all the women of New Zealand, including their own wives and girlfriends, were secretly in love with Imran: this was certainly the case if your present historian's own anecdotal evidence is anything to go by.

So there we were in the 1990s, sporting-wise, crapping out all over the place (unless you were among the diminishing band of Auckland rugby fans who even bothered to go down to Eden Park to witness the ritual demolition of brave but doomed sides from South of the Bombay Hills, or north of Albany, or across the Harbour Bridge). Meanwhile, the hand of the Great Helmsman, patted reassuringly by Bill Birch, was steering us unerringly towards the rocky cliffs, icebergs and coral reefs of MMP.

Chapter Eight

MMP:
or a Merry Mix-Up

*N*ational came into office in 1990 with a hidden agenda. In fact it was exactly the same agenda as that of the outgoing Labour Government: what National hid from the electorate was that they were actually the More of the Same Party and not, as they portrayed themselves, the Bring Back the Good Old Days Party. So when they upped, instead of repealing, the superannuation surcharge, wrapped their limbs even tighter round Don Brash than Labour had, and put the Business Roundtable at the wheel of the heavy roller smoothing out the level playing field, a mood of disillusionment settled on the electorate. It seemed to most voters that in a two-party 'first-past-the-post' system, it was the politicians who were first past the post, while the voters broke at the start and ended up nowhere. A Royal Commission, established by Labour, had recommended that some form, *any* form, of proportional representation was better than what pertained at that time; and the National Government, honouring a Labour promise, held a referendum on the issue in September 1992.

What the voters were offered, if they rejected FPP, was a choice between the German system of MMP (Muddled Member Parliament), and STV (Sexually Transmitted Voting). MMP allowed you to vote for an electorate MP, plus a party list. The number of list votes would determine how large a party would bulk in the new Parliament. To take a simple example, if a party got 40 per cent of the list vote and captured twenty electorate seats (still voted for on FPP principles), then it would get twenty-five list MPs as well. Or if it captured forty electorates, the 40 per cent of the list votes would mean that it would have only five list MPs. A subtle system, and no doubt Germans such as Hegel and Heidegger, not to mention Husserl and Haber (the inventor of poison gas), would have understood it, but not many New Zealanders did or do. But they were so pissed off with what happened under Muldoon (tyranny of the population by the Minister of Finance,) and Lange (tyranny of the population by the Minister of Finance), that they voted for it anyway.

The STV alternative was even harder to understand than MMP, and most voters took the acronym to stand for Sex on Television, which they were in favour of in the privacy of their own homes, but not as a means of electing the government. (Sex on

ALBERT EINSTEIN - YOUR SPECIALIST SUBJECT IS MMP. YOU HAVE TWO MINUTES STARTING FROM NOW...

television is not a good idea anyway: if the missionary position is adopted the top of the cabinet is too small, with consequent orthopaedic risks, and if a kneeling position is adopted, only the male partner gets to see what is on-screen.)

Anyway and whatever, the voters opted in September 1992 for MMP. This system was legislatively enacted in August 1993 and reaffirmed in the November 1993 General Election. We have now had our first General Election conducted within this framework. From now on, our politicians will find themselves slipping between the satin sheets with strange bedpersons. Parliament will reflect our electoral make-up, a consummation devoutly to be wished. Ordering a disordered democracy is what democracy is all about. Look at Italy, whose GNP is greater than Britain's. Look at Australia, which has long had a weird form of PR, and where the Queen's representative was able to turf out a democratically elected government. We are in for some lively times.

And rightly so. New Zealanders keep misleading themselves by thinking they are like propertied citizens of the nineteenth century. In fact, we are much more like the above-mentioned Italians, electorally: we don't know what we think from one minute to the next. But whatever we think from one minute to the next will now determine the composition of our Parliament. What larks! If democracy cannot be entertaining, then what is the point of it? We might as well go in for Stalinism, which we quite frequently used to do.

Mostly About Winston Peters

But not entirely. It should be recorded that in December 1991 the Alliance Party, dominated by Jim Anderton's New Labour, was formed, and the top fell off Mt Cook. Were these two events related? Certainly the loss of the top of Mt Cook was a bitter blow to those who had not yet ascended the mountain; they would never climb quite as high as those who had achieved the summit when it was still in one piece. On the other hand, a mountain which allows part of its top to fall off is less disruptive to air traffic than a mountain like Ruapehu, which fills the atmosphere with ash; so there is an upside to the downside of Mt Cook's diminution. The Alliance had no policy on the shrinkage of Mt Cook, but with its constituent parties – Greens, Democrats, Liberals, New Labour, Mana Motuhake – it had policies on almost everything else, and its personable leader, Anderton, would have blamed the loss of several feet off the top of Mt Cook on the National Government, had he not been persuaded otherwise by the pros in the smoke-filled back room, who felt that Mt Cook, or at any rate the top of it, was a bit of a grey area.

But the political Ruapehu of the years 1990-93 was Winston Peters. Journalists kept writing him off, declaring 'Winnie's finished this time', only to find him emitting fresh clouds of ash and smoke and not just from the cigarettes he constantly consumed. In September 1991 he was sacked as Minister of Maori Affairs. In June 1992 he began alleging that big business was influencing government policy-making. In October 1992 he was expelled from the National Party. Between 1992 and 1994 he attempted to table the so-called 'wine box' documents, which had to do with creative tax schemes drafted by Auckland lawyers and accountants using for their purposes a company called Euro-Pacific and a small Pacific country called the Cook Islands. These manoeuvres attracted a great deal of attention, and eventually resulted in the setting up of the 'wine box inquiry', of which more later.

But they kept Winston's charismatic profile and handsome head of hair (the equivalent in our politics of Margaret Thatcher's swirling hairdo) before the public. Superannuitants loved him because he promised to repeal the loathed surcharge. Maori loved him because he showed what could be achieved by wearing a snappy suit, instead of a gang patch. One of the reasons Doug Myers, chairman of the Business Roundtable, so loathes Winston, one suspects, is because Winston wears the same kind of suit as Doug does, and no worse cut. And lots of people liked Winston because he conveyed a sense of life's possibilities: he could be funny and corrosively rude, and didn't seem to be afraid of anybody. He was like a brown Bob Jones with more hair. There is a strand in the New Zealand character which responds to people who are openly rude about other people, especially if the ruderies are delivered with an engaging grin by a man who is clearly heterosexual and doesn't mind being seen smoking in public. Everyone who can't stand Helen Clark likes Winston. George Orwell wrote of 'the smelly little orthodoxies which contend for our souls'. There is nothing orthodox about Winnie, and that is why journalists and politicians consistently fail to get a handle on him. They regard him as dangerous because they can't work out where he is coming from. Where he is coming from is the folks back home.

Chapter Nine

'The Doctor is Sick!
Send for a Manager!'

One of the major upheavals in New Zealand society during the early 1990s was the so-called 'health reforms', overseen by the extremely fit Ruth Richardson, the rather less fit Simon Upton and the well-built Jenny Shipley. These involved the 'customer', i.e. a sick person, having to pay for the privilege of acquiring medicines from a chemist, advice from a GP, or cluttering up and ruining the smooth administration of a hospital. Labour had introduced something called Area Health Boards: they smelled far too strongly of democracy and were quickly chloroformed by National. Instead, we got something called 'a funder/provider split'.

Hospitals were no longer about helping you get better, or helping you to die, if that was the direction in which you were headed. They were reconstituted as Crown Health Enterprises, with the emphasis on the 'Enterprise' rather than the 'Health'. They were to be seen as stand-alone health supermarkets, competing with each other – and with GPs, midwives, nurses, specialists, pharmacists, psychologists and herbalists – for the health dollar dished out by their local Regional Health Authority. The RHA was the 'funder'; the various medical institutions or practitioners were the 'providers'. This was supposed to promote competition and efficiency. In fact it promoted brutality, ignorance and greed on a scale never before seen in this country, while an entirely new brand of medical bureaucrats helped themselves to the 'provisions'. People, 'customers', were refused treatment, turfed out to die, or simply told to bugger off. Nurses who had devoted their lives to mastering their profession were humiliated and made to feel less important than the accountant with an MBA and a BMW who ordered them about. Clinicians were excluded from any say in the administration of hospitals. A satisfactory 'outcome' for a hospital was not the number of lives it improved or eased; it was a profit in a balance sheet. It was and is madness, and madness is a condition not cured simply by a short, sharp jolt of MMP. For some time to come, the MBA/BMW set will still have life-and-death power over us, and charge us for the privilege of being managed by them.

The health reforms are like Rogernomics: we didn't know they were going to do it to us until they actually did it to us, and once they had done it to us, we didn't know what to do about it. New Zealanders like to trust their hospitals and their doctors, and find it hard to believe that the hospitals, in particular, are now being run like a car yard: if it doesn't move, unload it.

Let us light upon a lighter subject, that of auctions. In March 1993 a 167-kilogram blue-fin tuna was caught off the Bay of Plenty and subsequently sold at auction in Japan for $410,000. That must mean something. And in the same year a Colin McCahon painting, entitled 'I consider all the acts of oppression', was sold at auction in Auckland for $467,000. Just think what it might have fetched if a blue-fin tuna had been swimming around in the top right-hand corner. Clearly the arts of blue-fin tuna fishing and of painting with words written all over the painting, were alive and well in New Zealand. In May 1993 Jane Campion's film, *The Piano*, won the Palme d'Or at Cannes. Your present historian, ever with an eye to the main chance, approached the New Zealand Film Commission with a proposal for a film called *The Piano Accordion*, about a piano accordion carried into dense bush by Maori, and subsequently played to Bruno Lawrence by a lady with no clothes on. Would you believe the Film Commission turned this down? Well, you better had, because they did. Such is the life of the creative artist in a small country.

And it was not improved by the advent of TV3, which started off with a hiss and a roar of fireworks over Rangitoto in 1989, and went into receivership shortly thereafter. It survived, and eventually thrived. But the major televisual event of the early 1990s was the advent, to almost universal derision, of TVNZ's *Shortland Street*. We laughed at it, and

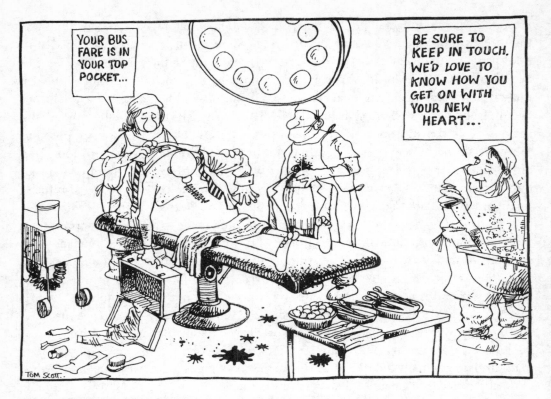

then found our kids watching it, and then we started watching it ourselves. Its basic premise was that our lives were safe in the hands of health professionals, all of whom were having sex with each other. Sample dialogue:

Doctor (male): Will you sleep with me?

Nurse (female): What kind of a question is that?

Doctor: Well, we *have* just saved this patient's life.

Patient: No, you haven't. I'm feeling a bit crook, actually. By the way, you have lovely breasts.

Doctor: How can you tell? I'm wearing a white coat.

Patient: Pardon me. It's just that my life is hanging by a thread.

Doctor (to Nurse): Is this guy some kind of a homosexual?

Nurse: Does that mean he has no rights under the Human Rights Act?

Patient: Good question, Doc. How do you answer that one?

The formula proved a winner. Once again, we are leading the world in issue-based soaps. (Remember *Close to Home*? If it was 5 November, they would have an episode about the dangers of fireworks.) *Shortland Street* holds up a mirror to society; admittedly, one of those fairground mirrors which make you look funny as you walk towards or away from them, but a mirror nevertheless.

Other matters which occurred between 1990 and 1993 which are worth rounding up in a chapter like this

In April 1992 President Mitterrand announced that he was suspending French nuclear testing in the Pacific. This did not make him popular in France, least of all among his own military leaders, but the people of the Pacific were fairly enthusiastic about it, and it showed how much French attitudes had changed since the days of the *Rainbow Warrior*, only seven years before. It was a considerable victory for everybody in the world who wasn't actually insane, a category which did not, unfortunately, include the Chinese, who carried on testing inscrutably. Perhaps they thought that nuclear weapons were only a slight extension of gunpowder, which they had invented centuries ago. Nobody complained about gunpowder: indeed the rest of the world adopted it with enthusiasm. So why should anybody complain about a bomb test? The Chinese think differently from us, and it is best not to think too much about the way they think.

As we know now, the suspension of testing was not to last, but we all enjoyed it while it did. Both National and Labour claimed credit for it; claims rather akin to the famous 'We Have Warned the Czar' editorial of a Hokitika newspaper during the Russian scare of 1877. But when the French did resume testing, in 1995, they discovered that not just the Pacific but world opinion was against them, and after conducting six pointless tests they flagged the whole thing away again.

Where New Zealand can claim credit is in taking a case to the International Court of Justice at The Hague, which resulted in the 1996 decision of that Court that nuclear weapons are illegal, except in certain circumstances of self-defence. The New Zealand case was argued by its Attorney-General, Paul East, elevated to the rank of QC especially for the occasion. But the true hero was Harold Evans, a Christchurch magistrate, who retired from the bench in 1977 because of increasing deafness, and for the next twenty years conducted a one-man campaign to persuade the New Zealand Government to mount a case in the court. He is a shining example of what can be achieved by a single person who believes that the law can liberate as well as oppress.

In 1992 the police were merged with traffic officers. The police hated it because they had always considered themselves superior to traffic officers, indeed regarded traffic officers as failed policemen. Traffic officers hated it because they resented the police opinion of them and anyway had no wish to view dismembered bodies or take details of burglaries that would never be cleared. The uneasy marriage has been recognised as a failure with a recent announcement that specialist units are to be set up within the police to deal with traffic matters, i.e. traffic officers.

In July 1992, thousands of lambs died in blizzards that coated Otago and Canterbury in snow. And in August 1992, there was another death which had nothing to do with snow and more to do with a broken heart, that of Sir Robert Muldoon.

The old boy had specific medical problems, but he never really got over the '84 defeat, his relegation to the back benches, and the realisation after 1990 that Bolger, Birch and Richardson were in his eyes just as bad as Lange, Douglas and Prebble. He spent his later years turning out self-justifying books, and performing memorably in *The Rocky Horror Show*, which would not have been a bad description for most of his Cabinets. Many still miss him, and certainly a Muldoon Budget night, compared with a Birch Budget night, is like a Janis Joplin concert compared with Dame Kiri singing in the Auckland Domain when the water has got into the sound system. At his peak, he frightened and excited us. But once we conquered our fear, the excitement disappeared as well. 'Politics and sex are aspects of each other,' as J-P Sinartre has aphoristically remarked.

Nineteen ninety-three was a year topped and tailed by two remarkable events. In the election of 6 November 1993, which we will deal with in the next chapter, National's huge majority disappeared, Labour came close to winning, and the Alliance and New Zealand First picked up two seats each. And in January 1993, a group of trampers in the Arthur's Pass region of the Southern Alps reported a sighting of a moa. They produced a photograph of the creature, which they claimed was a moa, and which scoffers said was the rear end of a deer. In this work, the moa thesis is opted for. After all, the takahe was not rediscovered until 1948: why should a moa not be sighted in 1993? It is comforting to think that there are still moa out there. But strain as he might, your present historian cannot discern a link between the moa-sighting of January and the political upheaval of November. One night, however, with a glass of mellow Scotch in his hand, the connection will come to him.

Chapter Ten

Through the Electoral Pain Barrier

*Y*ou don't have to be a big nation to be a divided one. Rwanda and Burundi have proved that. On 6 November 1993, New Zealand divided itself rather more pacifically. The Government and the Opposition achieved the same number of seats, if you assumed that New Zealand First and the Alliance were in the Opposition. Mike Moore, apparently assuming that he had won, made a vengeful speech addressed to Jim Bolger personally. Bolger, to his credit, accepting that his government had been derailed, made a statesmanlike speech promising the wet bus ticket of firm government. His dilemma was resolved within days, when Peter Tapsell, Labour Maori MP, broke ranks to become Speaker, thereby giving National a presumed majority of one.

Tapsell was despised by Labour for what he did. But, given what was about to happen in the Labour Party, wouldn't you do the same? The long knives were unsheathed shortly after the election and plunged into the ample back of Mike Moore, a man who had led his party from an impossible position in 1990 to the verge of victory in 1993. Not good enough, Mike, old boy. Sorry, but this is politics. Moore was dumped and replaced by two of the least charismatic politicians in our history: Helen Clark and David Caygill. One is bald; the other kept unsuccessfully changing her hairstyle. It was her unconvincing smile she should have worked on. Except that she couldn't. Those things have to be spontaneous if they are to work before the electorate. People liked Muldoon's 'heh-heh' chuckle because it was an expression of the man. David Lange always sounded as though he was laughing at everything he said, but at least the laughter was genuine: he was amused by his own wit. Bolger's smile has an infuriating air of self-satisfaction about it, but we accept that on the Richter Scale of self-satisfaction and non-introspection Jim reads between 7.9 and 9.4. And Winston, as has already been observed, can't keep a straight face for very long, so the grin is genuine.

But Helen is a serious woman. She surrounded herself with even more serious women. And if it is a cliché or quiché, that real men don't eat quiche, it is equally a cliché, and equally true, that serious women don't smile. For serious women, everything in life is an issue, and every issue is a serious issue. Why political women should be so much more serious than their male counterparts is a mystery. Ann Hercus was an exception; but when you think of Helen, Ruth and Jenny, you think of faces as full of fun as those of the American presidents carved into Mt Rushmore. To be sure, Bill Birch or Roger Douglas could give the girls a run for their money in the solemnity stakes. But somehow solemnity seems more noticeable when women exhibit it (no doubt a patriarchal slur we will in due course have to justify to the Human Rights Commission).

The years 1993-96 were to see our political geomorphology transformed, as parties struggled to be born or reborn, as the case may be. Irrespective of the question of the leadership of Helen Clark, Labour went into a decline. This had to do with the inability of the two parties of the Left, Labour and the Alliance, to form, or at any rate entertain the prospect of, a super-Alliance. The poisoned relationship between Clark and Anderton, formerly close friends, saddened observers who saw in it an analogy to what happens when marriages fall apart. And neither party could agree on how or when to form a coalition. The Alliance maintained that its twelve principles were inviolate, thereby making the Alliance sound rather like a political version of Alcoholics Anonymous. Any party which wished to coalesce with it would have to accept the twelve principles before the election. Labour took the view that it was best to have the election and then talk about coalitions. So the Alliance was saying, 'I won't sleep with you unless you sleep with me *before* I have slept with you' and Labour was saying 'I won't sleep with you until after I have slept with you and decided whether I *want* to sleep with you.'

National had a different problem. It was clearly going to need coalition partners.

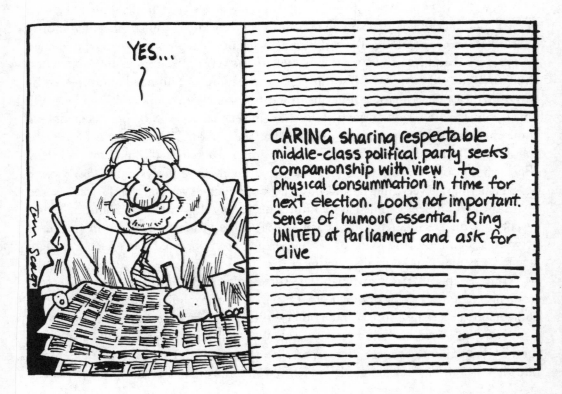

But its likely partners were political dwarves: ACT, Ross Meurant's ROC, and the various Christian Martyr parties. And the thing about dwarves, as no doubt Snow White could attest, is that you can satisfy them but they can't satisfy you. In the middle of all this confusion was New Zealand First, or Winston Peters, to give it its correct name, roaring up and down the polls like a yo-yo and confusing everybody. The market, that quivering, tremulous organism, was terrified of both the Alliance and New Zealand First. The public, or that portion of it which responded to polls, thought little of ACT or ROC or the Christians longing to cross the River Jordan. And neither National nor Labour could suggest mating with each other without losing huge amounts of support; even though, as couples who have been married a long time are said to do, they had come to look increasingly like each other.

So during 1995 and 1996, there were new parties surfacing from the mudpool of Parliament and disappearing with a 'plop'; and parties as alike as peas in a pod frantically trying to differentiate themselves from each other; as well as Labour, guiltily disavowing Rogernomics, and National, claiming credit for the results of Rogernomics but guiltily pretending not to have broken any promises. By the time these words are read, the voters will have decided, like cricket umpires, which parties deserve the uplifted finger; and which parties joyfully observe the fatal digit immobilised within the trousers.

Enough of politics. Let us turn to subjects more readily comprehensible, like

erections. In February 1994, work began on the Auckland Casino's Sky Tower. As these words were written, it is still clawing its way skyward. Many Aucklanders believe it has already developed a tilt to the left or the right, depending on where you view it from (rather like National, Labour or New Zealand First, depending on where you view *them* from). Barry Hickell, tutor in Creative Writing at the University of Auckland, composed a poem on the subject which was widely admired by his eager students:

> O Sky Tower, Auckland's lofty *éminence grise*,
> Climbing above our city's waters, hills, volcanoes and trees;
> Symbolising, as you pierce the clouds,
> The hopes and dreams of the milling crowds,
> Losing their money at the pokies and the table,
> Truly a modern Tower of Babel,
> Inching your way towards Eternity,
> Expression of Auckland's new modernity.
>
> Below you the sails; above you the stars;
> Around you restaurants, nightclubs, bars.
> Paris and Sydney have towers variously
> Designed; now Auckland must be taken seriously
> As a World City; we'll be thought of highly,
> Thanks to the soaring Tower of Brierley.
> Tourists will cry, 'Best tower we've been on,
> Even if it *has* got a bit of a lean on.'

Another building of which the country has every right to be proud is the Ohakea Air Force Base Commander's house, refurbished, as was revealed in March 1994, at a cost of $632,454. There was a bit of a fuss about this, but it is hard to see why. We don't want the Ohakea Air Force Base Commander to live in a poilite garage, do we? Of course we don't. After all, he has to entertain Australian and Indonesian colleagues. We don't want the Australians or Indonesians laughing at our Air Force behind our backs. The fuss was mean-spirited in your present historian's opinion. The sum involved was but a fraction of what was spent on the refurbishment of Parliament. And what is more important: a gilded talking-shop for politicians, or a front-line warrior's domestic comfort? There can be only one answer.

Whatever pleasure they drew from the protracted tumescence of the Sky Tower was somewhat diminished for Aucklanders when they discovered in June 1994 that they were running out of water. A dry autumn and winter had left their reservoirs almost empty. There was talk of a multi-million-dollar pipeline to draw water for Auckland from the mighty Waikato, but the various cities which make up Auckland couldn't agree, and Maori, who are rather sensitive on the subject of the Waikato, began dark mutterings. So Aucklanders, resourceful people, showered with a friend, did the dishes less often, put bricks in their toilet cisterns and lemonade in their Scotch. There was much talk of draining rainwater from roofs: the problem here was that little or no rain was falling to be drained. But before deaths from dehydration began to occur, and Bob Harvey, Mayor of Waitakere, chief opponent of the pipeline, was charged with manslaughter, the rains returned, ruining the spring, the lakes filled, and the guilty pleasures of the solitary shower or the aqueous hedonism of the bath could be indulged in once more. Still the episode was a reminder that Nature can withdraw as well as bestow her favours, and that if it hasn't rained, you can't water the garden even though that is the very reason why you want to water the garden. (This is known as 'Harvey's Paradox'.)

Nineteen ninety-four was memorable for the rise and fall of republicanism within New Zealand. An early manifestation was the spraying of Prince Charles with air freshener by an ardent (and presumably fragrant) anti-monarchist. The Prince took this pretty well, but was presumably less pleased when his mother's Prime Minister, Jim Bolger, began floating the idea that her Dominion of New Zealand was inevitably headed down the purple path to a Presidency. The Australian Prime Minister, Paul Keating, had opened up this debate in Australia (and look what happened to *him*). Jim is, of course, proud of his Irish ancestry, and, as is well-known, the Irish have no great fondness for the British Crown. Perhaps Jim thought he might be able to achieve in New Zealand what had not so far come about in Ulster, i.e. the breaking of British power. Anyway, it was not to be. His own National Party was deeply shocked and everyone else was mildly amused, except Maori, who are deeply attached to the Crown which so richly compensates them for its past perfidies. The episode demonstrated that, contrary to what Jim thinks, we actually like being a monarchy. We may be contemptuous of Fergie and deeply divided over Charles and Diana, busily engaged in spraying each other with CRC, but we like our dear old Queen, and the thought of the sort of ex-politician who might become Head of State fills most of us with horror. (Bolger? Birch? Richardson? Prebble? The mind blenches, blanches, flinches.) So what if our next monarch may be crowned in Westminster Abbey with the Orb in one hand and a tampon in the other? At least he has known the love of a good woman. It is just a pity she wasn't his wife.

Chapter Eleven

The Winebox:
A Very Short Chapter

Until the Winebox Commissioner of Inquiry, Sir Ronald Davison, delivers his findings, it is not possible to write as an historian about this fascinating judicial process, nor to draw conclusions from evidence yet to be given. And even when those findings are released they will be subject to motions for judicial review and appeals therefrom that will drag on for years: witness what happened with the Erebus Inquiry. To write of the Winebox now would be like drawing premature conclusions from evidence at the Erebus Inquiry without knowing what was going on in Mr Justice Mahon's mind. However, your historian was present at two sessions of the Winebox Inquiry, thereby becoming a witness to the unfolding of History, and attaches, as Appendix A, an account of the proceedings he wrote for *Metro* magazine. This is done for two reasons: one to give you, gentle reader, something of the flavour of the occasion; and two, because this is a work of scholarship, and works of scholarship, if they are to be taken seriously, must have a scholarly apparatus, such as footnotes, appendices, bibliographies and lengthy lists of acknowledgements to librarians. As this is a work intended for the general reader, and not for academics whittling away at the walls of their ivory towers, we have scrapped most of the above, but to show that we could do this sort of stuff if we wanted to, we annex Appendix A. (Appendix B, dealing with the police use of cellmates as secret witnesses in trials which are looking a bit flaky, has been restrained by High Court injunction.)

Chapter Twelve

The Mountain Speaks
(But What Is It Trying To Tell Us?)

*T*n September 1995, Mt Ruapehu erupted, covering large parts of the North Island with ash, hurling rocks into the air at the speed of sound, and reminding any of us who needed reminding that the earth's crust is very, very thin and that there is more to the Pacific Rim than expanding Asian economies. It was hard to tell whether the mountain was angry or just showing off. The eruptions continued into 1996, exciting vulcanologists but depressing the motel proprietors of Ohakune, carrot capital of the South Pacific. In whichever way one interprets Ruapehu, its eruptions and our frequent earthquakes remind us that we are perched on the skin of a swollen balloon, and from time to time Nature pricks it. We read of colossal natural disasters in other countries and try to suppress the reflection that it is going to be our turn sooner or later. We try to cheer ourselves up with the thought that Australia hasn't got any volcanoes – how they must envy us! – but it is a meagre consolation. The suppressed fear of earthquakes and volcanoes is a strand of our national subconscious which has been insufficiently explored by psychologists. At what psychic cost do we bury this fear and carry on as though we were living in Scotland or Bavaria? One of the few writers to deal with this issue is the Wellington playwright Hope Glimmer, whose play, *Waiting for the Big One*, opens as follows:

Scene: The exterior of a Wellington art cinema; a queue outside it rather like the one in Annie Hall. *We observe two characters in the queue:* MEL, *a Woody Allen lookalike and* JO, *a Diane Keaton lookalike.*

MEL: Of course, Tarantino isn't exploiting violence as such. What he is doing is making us laugh at our fascination with it.
JO: Mel…
MEL: He's obviously influenced by the Brechtian *Verfremdumseffekt* – the distancing…
JO: Mel…
MEL: To suggest that he's exploiting violence ignores –

JO: Mel, I don't want to go in there.

MEL: What?

JO: I don't want to go in there. What if there's an earthquake?

MEL: What are you talking about?

JO: It'd be awful to be in a theatre if there was an earthquake.

MEL: Who says there's going to be an earthquake? Who've you been talking to?

JO: I just have a feeling there's going to be an earthquake and I want to go home.

MEL: Home? We live in Wadestown, for God's sake. If there *was* an earthquake, we'd probably end up in Thorndon, buried under millions of tons of rubble.

JO: All right – let's go to Somes Island.

MEL: Look, you can't just *go* to Somes Island. You have to get permission. Anyway, it's full of diseased animals. We might catch something.

JO: Well, where *shall* we go?

MEL: In here. To see Tarantino's *Aqueduct Ferrets*. Apparently, the catharsis is phenomenal, awesome. The pre-title sequence –

JO: I'm leaving you.

MEL: Where are you going?

JO: Somewhere I feel safe. Tierra del Fuego.

MEL: Tierra del Fuego? Safe? It's covered in volcanoes. That's what the name means – 'Land of Fire'.

JO: Maybe. But I'll bet they don't show Tarantino movies there.

In the event Mel and Jo do go home, drink heavily and bicker wittily, there *is* an earthquake and they do end up in Thorndon buried under millions of tons of rubble. (This is suggested by lighting, sound and large pieces of polystyrene painted grey.) Most audiences leave silently and for the next few days a bus going past the house can send them into panic attacks. But at least Glimmer's work confronts us with the fact that for far too long earthquakes have been swept under the carpet.

There were other eruptions beside Ruapehu in 1995. In February, there were disgraceful scenes at Waitangi, on the celebration of our national day. Maori protesters spat at the Governor-General, Dame Cath Tizard. The New Zealand flag was trampled on. Attempts were made to collapse a grandstand. Hate-filled faces glared from behind tattoos. No individual was killed, but the day itself was. The 1996 ceremony took place behind closed doors. And rightly so. A national day, the advent of which fills most people with dread and some people with hate, is best abandoned. And a nation which cannot even enjoy its own national day is better off introspecting quietly rather than celebrating publicly.

In March, Maori, led by a rancorous man called Ken Mair, a renegade sailor, occupied a park in Wanganui. Mair claimed not to recognise the authority of the Crown or Maori elders or anybody at all except the news media. They, for their part, did him the honour of taking him seriously, an honour he did not deserve. Most people, including your present historian, thought he should have been arrested for trespass and sentenced to a media blackout. The occupation ended after seventy-nine days but not before cars had been attacked and their occupants threatened by oppressed and downtrodden gang members.

Maori and their politically correct supporters achieved another media victory when the Chief Government Whip, John Carter, was forced to resign after a prank. Pretending to be a Maori called Hone, he rang his colleague John Banks's radio talkback programme and made some bad jokes behind the mask of this character. He certainly showed bad judgement in going on the Banks show under any name and the banality of the jokes meant his downfall was deserved. Comic impersonation is best left to comedians. Banks's programme has been a continual thorn in the side of his Cabinet colleagues. It gives Banks a chance to rant and to say twice – *to say twice* – what is not worth saying once.

At the other end of the radio spectrum is Kim Hill's nine to noon session on the National Programme. Hill is quick-witted, articulate and often witty. But although almost half her audience are men (presumably masochistic men or retired men who don't like pop music), she never loses a chance to put men down. On the Kim Hill programme, 1970s feminism is alive and well. But much of the show consists of a dreary parade of counsellors, alternative medicine practitioners, faxes from hypochondriacs and grizzles from aggrieved parents of school children. However, she can be funny with Gary

McCormick and elicits the occasional interesting opinion from Sir Geoffrey Palmer, a considerable feat.

For the Left, 1995 was not a good year. Because of profound crises in his family life, Jim Anderton kept coming and going as leader of the Alliance. The nation continued not to warm to Helen Clark and most Labour supporters, apart from his caucus colleagues and Clark herself, would have preferred to see Mike Moore back in the top job. But since Clark wouldn't make way for him and since he didn't have the numbers to roll her, he brooded on the back benches. Winston Peters' apotheosis was not to come about until 1996. So this left the field clear for Jim Bolger and 1995 was certainly his year. When the French resumed nuclear testing at Moruroa, he was able to present himself as an anti-nuclear champion, to the fury of all who recalled his past support for ANZUS and ship visits. The CHOGM conference and the consequent presence in our midst of Nelson Mandela enabled him to embrace the great man and present himself as a determined foe of apartheid, to the fury of all who remembered his presence in Muldoon Cabinets and support of the '81 Springbok tour. The hanging of Ken Saro-Wiwa and eight others gave Bolger a chance to reveal himself as a fighter for freedom and justice in Nigeria. Everything he touched turned to gold and there seemed to be nothing that anybody could do about it, except grind their teeth in impotent rage.

In 1995, the police shot two mad people in quick succession. There was little else

they could have done in the particular circumstances of each case but a mental health system which relies upon the police killing people the system isn't treating adequately can hardly be said to be exercising a care-giving function. A report was commissioned from retired judge Ken Mason. It recommended spending a whole lot more money on mental health. Whether its recommendations will be implemented and, if implemented, whether they will make any difference, remains to be seen… The worldwide fashion for keeping mentally ill people in the community is seen as beneficial by psychiatrists and governments alike. But it results in deranged people killing themselves or being killed by police, and parents living in mortal terror of their schizophrenic children. 'Incarceration' is an ugly word, but so are 'suicide' and 'murder'.

The Culture of Sport and The Sport of Culture

For many New Zealanders, 1995 will glow in the memory forever because it was the year we won the America's Cup. Peter Blake's *Team New Zealand* obliterated all the challengers' challenges and then defeated Dennis Conner's *Stars and Stripes* five-nil. This was accomplished not just by brilliant design and celestial seamanship, but also by the wearing of red socks. (It still seems surprising that some quick-witted entrepreneur did not seize the opportunity to flood the market with red condoms: a condom, after all, is only a sock of a different kind.) Hysterical victory parades greeted the Cup's arrival in New Zealand and Blake was knighted almost before he stepped off 'Black Magic' and into history. The

Cup triumph enabled us to forget the woes of our cricket team, a young team inclined to knee injuries, rampant egoism and the smoking of dope at barbecues (presumably in the hope that the smell of charred sausages would smother the aroma of marijuana). Geoff Howarth, the coach, was dumped and his replacement, Glenn Turner, despite having turned the team's fortunes around by prodding them into winning a few games, was also dumped in favour of Steve Rixon, an Australian.

Turner was accused by players and management of being bad at communicating with players. But under him, the players communicated with the public by playing some splendid innings. Clearly, this form of communication is regarded by New Zealand Cricket as less important than group psychotherapy: 'Cricket-As-Feeling'. Mr Rixon is apparently enormously popular with the teams he coaches: let us hope that the warm flow of emotion in the dressing-room percolates out to the long-suffering, battered and beleaguered New Zealand cricket supporter on the terraces. Your present historian is of the view that it doesn't matter two straws if the coach never speaks to the team and the team never speak to each other, so long as they take some wickets and make some runs. This New Age idea that membership of the New Zealand cricket team should somehow make you a better person is fatuous; and how can we take pride in any future victories, especially over Australia, if we have been coached by an Australian? Would we accept the idea of the All Blacks being coached by a South African? We may have to because the All Blacks are now

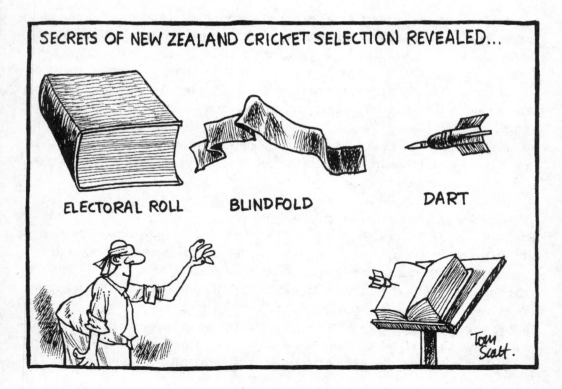

SECRETS OF NEW ZEALAND CRICKET SELECTION REVEALED...

ELECTORAL ROLL   BLINDFOLD   DART

owned lock, stock and television-camera-barrel by Rupert Murdoch and if he, in order to preserve his investment, says we should have a South African coach, then a South African coach is what we will have. Thanks to Murdoch, players now earn six-figure incomes and turn up on the covers of women's magazines, their nuptials eagerly dissected and displayed. Sure, it makes a change from endless covers of Rachel Hunter and Princess Di. But learning about All Blacks' private lives is scant compensation for the fact that none of their big games go live-to-air any more and the nation is divided into the 'have-Skys' and the 'have-Sky-nots'. (The latter have more fun, actually, because they watch the game at a pub.)

The sport of culture emerged with the increasing popularity of operatic concerts in the Auckland Domain or Hagley Park. They usually feature one of the two Dames-than-whom-there-is-nothing-like: Kiri and Malvina. Hundreds of thousands of people turned out for these concerts – far more than could ever be crammed into Eden or Lancaster Park. Brilliant sound engineering meant that you could hear Dame Kiri in Helensville and Dame Malvina in Ashburton. And being concerts, they were miles more fun than opera as such because you didn't have to put up with the ridiculous plots and the appalling acting. There is a strong argument for preserving theatrical opera, but only as a source of songs to be sung at open-air concerts. After all, at open-air concerts you can gnaw at a chicken leg and glug away at a bottle of chardonnay, behaviour frowned upon in the stalls of a theatre.

Talking of glugging, lots of it went on in the film *Once Were Warriors*, a Kiwi flick which gave the lie to the motto suggested for the New Zealand Film Commission, 'Once Were Audiences'. This drama of what police call 'domestics' captured the imagination of New Zealand audiences for reasons best left unexplored. (Men secretly admired Jake Heke and so did women, though everyone loudly deplored him.) The film achieved a limited success overseas but Arnold Schwarzenegger and Bruce Willis slept untroubled beside their swimming pools. The saddest cultural event of 1996 was the disbanding of the group Crowded House. It's understandable that they would all want rooms of their own but the house will certainly seem empty without them.

The Culture of Cultures

The outstanding political event of 1996 in the run-up to the election was the astonishing rise in pollular support for Winston Peters' New Zealand First Party. Peters touched on a nerve when he began attacking immigration policies which had seen substantial Asian immigration in recent years, particularly into Auckland. He didn't attack Asians as such but the public decided that he had and exhibited pollular preferences accordingly. Asians were unpopular, again particularly in Auckland, because people didn't like the architecture of the new houses they built and because of their allegedly bad driving. This was a bit rich coming from the nation which invented the weatherboard, tin-roofed bungalow and whose citizens had been killing each other on the roads at the rate of 700-800 a year before New Asians began arriving here. But there it was: Winston had struck a lost chord.

And the fact that most New Asians were peaceable, worked hard and their kids did well at school, only made the descendants of earlier waves of immigration dislike them all the more. The Dutch had encountered the same dislike forty years before. In immigrant societies, only the names are changed to renew the prejudices.

Chapter Thirteen

Ode to New Zealand:
or 'It's a Wrap!'

'It's a wrap' is a phrase beloved of all who work in film and television. It means the hard work – setting-up, shooting, sound recording – is over and the downstream stuff like editing and transmitting can begin. It also means a 'wrap' party, usually held in unappealing surroundings, during which relationships forged in the fires of adversity either temper into steel or melt like butter. The point, dear reader, of the analogy, is that this book is approaching its wrap and A. K. Grant and Tom Scott would love to invite you to a party but we haven't room. All we can offer instead are some concluding reflections and an ode to New Zealand.

The twelve years between 1984 and 1996 have seen an upheaval in New Zealand society unparalleled in our history. In 1984, New Zealand was not markedly dissimilar to the country as it existed in 1948. Certainly, unemployment was a great deal higher but we still had a regulated Welfare State; we were relatively egalitarian and the gulf between rich and poor had not widened into an abyss; there were plenty of post offices and commercials on TV were regarded as supportive of the medium rather than the main reason for it. In the years between 1984 and 1996, all has changed. To modify the French aphorism, 'Plus ça change, plus c'est something completely different'. Nowadays, we have wonderful restaurants and well-stocked foodbanks. The economy is controlled not by Parliament but by the Governor of the Reserve Bank. Inflows and outflows of capital are like the magma swelling up under Ruapehu: nobody knows when they're coming and nobody knows where they're going to. Our economy is on its back with its legs spread. Business news, crammed with meaningless decimal statistics, dominates the National Programme, punctuated by equally meaningless weather forecasts. Maori grievances, like balloons, inflate themselves with their own hot air; so do politicians. Farmers have passed from being protected to being a threatened species, with unforeseeable consequences for the gene pool. Most of us have more freedom and most of us have more debt. We are told that our economy is the envy of the Western world: if that is so, God knows what the other economies must be like. We are told by government and the Business Roundtable (more or less the same thing), that their vision is the only vision and that anybody seeing something else has not been taking their medication.

The 1984-96 era may come to be seen as a volatile interregnum between two periods of stability. Or it may be seen as the springboard from which we execute a perfect dive into the waters of the future. There is no way of knowing. But the fact that despite all the uproar and shouting of the past few years, we remain a fundamentally decent people justifies a fundamentally pessimistic satirist in penning the following ode:

To the People of New Zealand

> Just north of the great Southern Ocean
> Lies a land on Pacific's broad rim;
> Lapped by the waves' gentle motion
> And lit by the effulgent Jim.
> A turbulent, gentle society
> Inhabits this temperate clime;
> Riddled by placid anxiety;
> Ahead – only just – of its time.

Rifts and divisions exist in
The world's far-flung social laboratory.
Greed is a powerful piston,
Powering political oratory.
But most of us aren't that greedy,
On our own or on others' behalves.
We eat, when we're hungry and needy,
Hamburgers, not fatted calves.

The All Blacks, it's claimed, best express us,
But we aren't like them at all.
Selected, we'd make awful messes,
And always turn over the ball.
And anyway, All Blacks are jokers,
While half of the country is female:
They come from a quite different *locus*,
And transmit quite different e-mail.

New Zealanders ne'er will be helots.
We're too independent for that.
We're governed by dolts and by zealots,
And cats who are rather too fat.
But if, while their cellphones are bleeping,
We feel that we're sick of this club,
We'll send them back home, softly weeping,
And take someone else to the pub.

All it needs is a decent tune to go with it.

The End

Appendix A

Days of Wine and Winston
by A. K. Grant

In the sixties, the fundamental question was, 'Do you remember where you were when you heard that President Kennedy had been shot?' In the nineties, the equivalent question for journalists is 'Were you at the Winebox Inquiry when Winston Peters was on the stand?' Your correspondent, or 'I', as I prefer to refer to myself, was indeed there for three exhilarating days, which I would not have missed for quids, or their decimal equivalent. Unfortunately, I had to return to Christchurch to appear as barrister in a much less august forum, and so did not witness the collapse of the stout, or stocky party, when his mystery witness, Marcia Read, failed, as we lawyers say, to come up to brief. But for the three days that I *was* there, I was a privileged observer of a clash of cultures, legal and political, like ocean liners, colliding with each other, their lights blazing in the night, but neither of them holing each other below the waterline.

It began for me last year, on Monday 31 July, when Winston was months away from taking the stand, but when the Commission of Inquiry, having been becalmed for months, suddenly erupted like Mt Ruapehu (to mix a metaphor). The lava, or magma, or lahar, or whatever you call that stuff, was the evidence of John David Nash, a senior official in the IRD, or Incompetent Revenue Department, as Winston would like it to be known. The morning of 31 July dawned tranquilly in Auckland. In accordance with the precepts of the New Journalism, which puts the journalist at the centre of anything he writes about, I should record that I arose from the bed of a woman to whom I have been engaged for many years, cleaned my teeth and other parts of my body, had a Coke for breakfast, resisted the temptation to put some gin into it, draped myself in clean garments, both outer and under, and was driven by my consort to the National Mutual Centre in Shortland Street. There I ascended to the ninth floor, where an astonishing sight confronted my glaucous orbs.

It was like Houston Control in the heroic days of the moon missions. There were wall-to-wall VDUs, being stared at by wall-to-wall QCs. And, of course, the Commissioner had one, and so did the witness on the stand, or, to be accurate, the desk. It was utterly different from anything resembling an ordinary court. In an ordinary court, the lawyers look at the witnesses, the judge looks at the witnesses, the witnesses look at the lawyers, and in a jury case, the jury look at the lot of them. But here nobody looked at anybody. They all stared at their VDUs. It was as though none of them were actually there. They could have been scattered all over the country, linked by VDUs. It was trial by Virtual Reality.

Except that it wasn't. Reality intruded, both in July 1995, when Mr Nash took the stand, and in June 1996, when a certain dark-haired politician, aggressively coiffured, arrived to ringing cheers from busloads of adoring hip replacementees from Tauranga. But to go back to the earlier date: Mr Nash booted the Inquiry into a new and more fascinating dimension, to the great surprise of all of us on the press benches, when he said:

'I have always regarded the Carter Holt Harvey (CHH) unwind transaction as the most questionable in the "wine box"… it was necessary to discover the true facts and answer the analyses which had been put forward by CHH's lawyers. When I gave evidence in February 1995, some key facts remained uncertain and the legal analyses were still being considered. That work has now been completed and the suspicions arising from the "wine box" materials have been confirmed to the point of proof in the absence of further evidence. I believe the evidence points that in a key element the transaction was a sham which may involve tax evasion.'

Later he said, 'Careful investigation arising from, in part, the documents in the "wine box" has produced evidence which raises the question as to whether $63 million of income has been suppressed by the CHH group.'

And later still, he said: 'Further analysis and information has certainly altered my perception of some transactions.'

Well! Nash's evidence and the exhibits attached to it went on for several hundred pages. But those three extracts just quoted proved that Winston Peters had been right all along in claiming that the documents in the winebox smelt, not of wine, but of dead fish, and that a public inquiry was absolutely necessary. And that is still the case despite the reversal he suffered when he had to admit that he could not prove that the former Commissioner of Inland Revenue, David Henry, or the Director of the Serious Fraud Office, Charles Sturt, had been corrupted by David Richwhite or Sir Michael Fay. He went a bridge too far there. But his basic point has been made: that while the Cook Islands Government was receiving millions of dollars in aid from the New Zealand taxpayer, it was being used by companies and their lawyers and accountants in New Zealand to erode the New Zealand tax base by a substantial multiple of the aid being paid to it.

It was a good life if you were a Cook Islands Government minister or official in the late eighties. The next witness after John Nash was a Michael John Fleming. He was Secretary of the Treasury in the Cook Islands during 1987 and 1988. He told us somewhat plaintively that: 'The operation of the Cook Island tax haven was kept separate from Treasury. The Crown Law Office and Cook Islands Monetary Board were actively involved.

I did not know much about it.' But what he *did* know about was a wonderful device called 'the multiplier'. This was a per diem travelling allowance. As he explained it: 'The effect of the multiplier was that a Government minister or official who incurred expenses while on Government business overseas would receive payment of his costs multiplied by the multiplier applying to him. For example, if the Prime Minister stayed in a hotel in Paris that cost $1000 a night, he got paid $2500, as his multiplier was 2.5. I was against the multiplier… given a system like that people were encouraged to stay in the most expensive hotel that they could.' (And, of course, for as long as they could, and bear in mind, gentle reader, that the New Zealand taxpayer was footing the bill for much of this.) Fleming wrote papers suggesting that the multiplier should be reduced to reasonable levels. Readers with a healthy contempt for politicians will not be surprised to learn that '… the Cook Islands Government accepted my recommendations concerning the officials but did not accept my recommendations concerning ministers during my time'.

He also deposed that because of his opposition to the still uncompleted, Italian-financed tourist hotel, '… I received a threat from (a personal assistant of Norman George, the Minister in charge of the project), to the effect that if I did not support the proposal, harm could come to myself and my wife and children'.

Riveting stuff. I could not stay to hear more of it and returned to Christchurch, following with fascination the progress of the Inquiry through newspapers and the radio. But when it was announced that on 5 June 1996, the Tribune of the People, Winston

Peters, was to give evidence before his very own Tribunal, I suggested to the editor of *Metro* that it was time for me to attend again. He agreed with me, and so on the morning of Wednesday 5 June, I found myself once more on the ninth floor of the National Mutual Centre, waiting for the arrival of the People's Voice.

The view was rather more restricted on this occasion, from the press benches at any rate, for not only were there still wall-to-wall VDUs and wall-to-wall QCs: in front of the press benches, there were wall-to-wall TV cameramen and sound men, between whose legs and over whose shoulders we print journalists peered and peeped like prisoners being guarded by a line of police. (Most TV cameramen are very big; presumably something to do with the physical requirements of the job.) However, by dint of a certain amount of contortion, it was possible to get a view of the entertaining events which followed.

Just before Winston came in, I had speculated to Ian Wishart, a journalist who has covered the Inquiry from the beginning and indeed written a book on it, that when Winston entered it would be to an orchestral accompaniment; either 'The Entry of the Gladiators' or 'The Arrival of the Queen of Sheba'. As it turns out, it should have been 'There'll be Bluebirds Over the White Cliffs of Dover', because when he arrived, he was greeted by ringing cheers from the busloads of World War II generation New Zealand First supporters, many of them wearing New Zealand First cockades or lapel buttons, who packed the public gallery.

Winston was, as always, looking good; the well-cut suit and the even more well-cut dark and curly hair, with its promise of abundant virility; the impeccable shirt, tie, shoes and socks, and the sober mien unsuccessfully concealing the capacity for aggressive wit, only to be exercised, of course, on behalf of the ordinary people of New Zealand.

His counsel, Brian Henry, read out an opening statement and then Winston took the stand to read the brief of his own evidence. He did this well; he has a deep voice with a slight rasp in it, and his staccato delivery is softened by his habit of slurring his consonants. He doesn't always sound so crash-hot when he is bickering with Kim Hill or Mike Hosking (mind you, neither do they, when they are interrogating Winston; both sound as though they are mastering their fear of an interviewee at least as quick-witted as they are. Hosking's voice rises to a bat-like squeak and Hill's would too if it could get up that far). But the measured nature of proceedings where question and answer are being recorded by an absolutely brilliant courtroom typist suited Winston well; he quickly caught on to the house style adopted by all the QCs, which was to preface each question with, 'Mr... Peters, I suggest to you so-and-so.' Peters would respond in like vein. He got bested once in this game when, after having been hammered away at by Willie Young QC for a day and a half, he kept forgetting Bruce Squire's surname. He apologised for this; Squire was magnanimous. 'That's all right, Mr...?' he said to the best-known politician in the country, and turned to Young, as though seeking assistance. 'Peters,' said Young helpfully. There was much laughter from the press benches, and an engaging grin from Winston but little amusement from the patched members of Greypower '61 at the back of the room. It was a converted try to Squire but he didn't cross the line many times after that, as we shall see.

After Winston had finished reading his brief, the cross-examinations began. During the time that I was there, three QCs attempted to chase and pin down this elusive iron butterfly.

They exhibited a mixture of styles. Bruce Squire, for the IRD, resembled the Dormouse in *Alice in Wonderland*, not least because of his habit of peering into his papers and being told to keep his voice up. Rhys Harrison, for Fay Richwhite kept his voice up rather more than he needed to, and resembled Robespierre, convinced of his own and his client's rectitude. But no guillotine awaits him, and if he did go to it, it would be in a BMW, not a tumbrel. Willie Young for the SFO, the most computer-literate of the three, was also the most human: he lost his temper from time to time and sometimes resembled Captain Kirk of the Starship Enterprise, confronting an alien life-form. He was first out of the blocks and began his confrontation aggressively enough:

Q: Mr Peters, have you ever been accused of being corrupt?
A: Mr Young, I don't have an immediate memory of that, no.
Q: I imagine if you had been accused of being corrupt, you would probably recall it?
A: Not necessarily, Mr Young, it would depend on who made the allegation. I'm a politician.

That set the tone for much of what followed. For me, the most entertaining example of the clash of cultures between political streetfighter and legal aristocrat came at page 6324 of the notes of evidence (that gives you an idea of how long this thing has been going on):

A: … I meet people every day around this country, Mr Young. Possibly I have spoken to 180,000 in the last year at public meetings. I have not had one get up and say: Mr Peters, you should not be saying those awful things about the Serious Fraud Office.
Q: Perhaps you mix in the wrong company?
A: Well, if you regard the people of New Zealand as being the wrong company, I can understand that, given the circles *you* mix with. (Ringing cheers and release of balloons and pigeons from Hell's Superannuitants at the back of the room.)

I do not wish to give the impression that every question from Young was met with a witty, populist response from Winston. Several times, Young appeared to have Winston painted into a corner. But Winston would escape with a flying leap to a dry part of the floorboards, or sometimes into a different room altogether. And I don't think Young altogether made things easier for himself by his concentration on press releases. It was understandable that he should, since much of the war between Winston and Chas Sturt was conducted through press releases or press reports of speeches. But what often happened would be questioning about, say, a press release by Sturt, which had then been paraphrased in a press release by Winston. In the course of questioning from Young, Winston would paraphrase his earlier paraphrase, and then be asked whether the later paraphrase was a fair paraphrase of the earlier paraphrase, itself allegedly an unfair paraphrase of what Sturt had said in the first place. The head began to spin after several hours of this, and some of Winston's answers, not to mention some of Young's questions, began to take on an *Alice in Wonderland* quality, as at page 6297:

> Q: … Are there any particular media statements you are pointing to?
> A: I suppose one in particular was a request to the Serious Fraud Office to appear on the programme and their decline.
> Q: I see, so when you say media statements, you also include refusals to make media statements?
> A: When I say media statements, I mean statements to the media.
> Q: Including a refusal to make a statement?
> A: A refusal to make a statement is a statement to the media nevertheless.

There was lengthy and labyrinthine debate about whether the Serious Fraud Office has the power to investigate fraud or corruption in respect to a tax settlement where the allegation of fraud or corruption is against the IRD itself. Not a question to be answered in advance of the Commissioner's findings, and it seemed to me that a lot of the questioning of all three QCs was either a waste of time or unfair to Peters in this regard. They kept pressing him about matters which he could not answer because they were outside the terms of reference of the Inquiry.

Although, as I have said, Young was thoroughly the master of the video technology and kept, as he termed it, 'sending' documents from his screen to Winston's, even he was not immune from malfunction. He sent Winston a wiring diagram of something called the 'Patonga' transaction. When Winston got it, it was upside down. Not that that mattered very much because, although Winston called the transaction fraud, he wasn't able to explain what was fraudulent about it. He said he relied on his experts in that regard. Later on, when he got the diagram again, it was on its side. It seemed symbolic: these wine box transactions can only be understood if you are lying on your side or standing on your head (I mean no disrespect to the Commissioner when I say this).

Eventually, on the afternoon of the Thursday, Young decided he had gone about as far as he could go and Bruce Squire, for the IRD, rose to take over the assault. Comedy soon reared its unruly head. Squire was asking Winston about the 3 December 1991 agreement, between the investors in *Merry Christmas Mr Lawrence* and the IRD, which Winston alleges is evidence of corruption.

A: … I gave it the test commonly known in America as the duck test. If it looks like a duck, if it quacks like a duck and waddles like a duck and smells like one, I suggest it is a duck.

Q: Have you said that before, Mr Peters? Have you used those words before? Have you used those words before?

A: Not those precise words.

Q: Haven't you used those precise words in Parliament?

A: No, I have not. I'll tell you the difference. I have added in 'smells like a duck'.

Q: Very amusing, Mr Peters. I am sure we are all enjoying your sense of humour.

A: You *did* ask, Mr Squire.

Winston and Squire continued to spar through the rest of Thursday afternoon. Sometimes the Commissioner told Squire that he had brought an undesired answer on his own head; sometimes he told Winston to stick to the point and not trespass into forbidden territory.

One passage gave an interesting insight into the bacilli currently flourishing in New Zealand's political culture dish. Squire was questioning Winston about allegations of political interference in the *Mr Lawrence* settlement and suggested that Winston no longer supported that assertion. Peters said: 'When you have Cabinet colleagues telling you that you are "hurting our friends" or "they are going to bankrupt you" or "they are big boys, Winnie", you can be certain I am not going to withdraw allegations of political interference.'

Squire's persistence eventually paid off, largely as a result of Winston's inability to admit error and abandon a previously held position. There was a lengthy scrap about a phone conversation between John Nash of IRD and a Mr Papageorgiou, in charge of taxation matters for the BNZ. This conversation took place on 29 April 1994, at 3.30pm. Winston alleged, in effect, that someone had leaked to the IRD details of a press statement he was *about* to put out which contrasted the treatment of unemployed Fortex workers, for income assessment purposes, with what he saw as favourable treatment of the BNZ in respect of a 'captive insurance scheme', the details of which need not concern us here. The point is, Winston was alleging that somehow Nash had got wind of his statement before it was released and had alerted the BNZ to its impending emergence. Winston's problem, as it turned out, was that the little figures on top of a copy of the fax showed that it must have been in the hands of Wyatt Creech, Minister of Revenue, to whom Winston's office had copied it, by 2.28pm at the latest. So Nash of the IRD could have seen the statement before his phone call to Papageorgiou, without there being any question of bugging of, or treachery within, Winston's office. Instead of saying something sensible like: 'Well, that still leaves the question of why Nash was ringing Papageorgiou in the first place?' Winston demanded to see the original of the fax, suggesting that the figures at the top could have been 'doctored up'. This is nonsense, as anyone familiar with faxes knows.

There is an old principle of cross-examination which is that when you have discredited a witness, either by catching them out in a lie or, as in this case, made them look silly, that is a good time to sit down. Squire did so, thus allowing Rhys Harrison for Fay Richwhite, to rise to his feet.

Harrison has a head of hair almost as abundant as Winston's but I draw no particular conclusion from this. He has a piercing voice, fuelled, like Winston's, by anger, but in a rather more theatrical way. He got a lot further with Winston than the other QCs did, mainly because he was coming from a stronger position. He pressed Winston again and again for evidence that not only were Sturt and Henry corrupt but that they had been corrupted by Michael Fay and David Richwhite. Winston didn't have any, or at any rate none that he could introduce within the Inquiry's terms of reference. But he refused to modify his allegation, thus making his answers seem casuistical and devious. At one stage his counsel, Brian Henry, intervened on his behalf, but, on the Friday afternoon at any rate, the Commissioner was becoming irritated. He said, at page 6492: 'The problem with a lot of these questions, Mr Henry, is that Mr Peters is being asked as to what evidence he has relating to certain matters. Now if he has any hard evidence he can say so. If he has personally no knowledge of any evidence he can say that, or if he is relying on you to produce further evidence he can say that, but let's have a direct straightforward answer to each of the questions. As I see it, Mr Peters is trying to argue a case using any scrap of evidence he has come across or believes he has seen. Now, let's get down to some concrete facts.'

The 'scrap of evidence' to which the Commissioner was referring was that of a Ms Marcia Read, a former director of the Phobic Trust, who Winston said had contacted him after Sturt had given evidence that he had never met Fay or Richwhite, to say that she had been present at Fay's house when Sturt had turned up there and met the Fay babysitter, thereby establishing, in Winston's words, an 'acquaintanceship' between Sturt and Fay, an acquaintanceship previously denied on oath.

Interesting stuff, if supported by Ms Read. Not necessarily evidence of corruption or a conspiracy to defraud the Revenue, but evidence that the Director of the Serious Fraud Office had misled the Commissioner as to the level of his personal contact with Fay. But, alas for the people of New Zealand, when Ms Read did give evidence she said that she had never told Winston that she had been present at the Fay household when Sturt turned up.

The days of wine and Winston that I observed were a clash of two worlds: the world of 'What do you mean by…?' meeting the world of 'You know perfectly well what I mean'. The world of 'Please answer my question' meeting the world of 'Here's a question for you!' The world of 'Where's your evidence?' with the world of 'The people of New Zealand will answer that on October 12'. The world of 'I am exercising my considerable skills on behalf of my client' with the world of 'People want to vote for me, talk to me, touch me'.

Parallel universes, but one is a great deal more universal than the other. One is based on reason; one on belief. Human history suggests that belief is the more powerful: belief doesn't rest on reason but reason can be shaken by belief.

The Commission of Inquiry is enormously important, impeccably conducted and will deliver considered findings. But in the world outside, they have already been considered. Initially, the IRD and the SFO concluded that the wine in the wine box had not aged sufficiently. But the public, because of Winston Peters, have tasted it and concluded that it goes well with dead fish and cooked goose.

Wine is a central aspect of the Christian sacrament. It may well contribute to the sanctification of Winston Peters. But he should beware. Saints are inclined to come to gory ends.